CB082096

Mayta

Catapulta

SECTION_1_INTR
SECTION_2_MY_
SECTION_3_MAI
SECTION_4_POS
SECTION_5_26_
SECTION_6_MAY
SECTION_7_THE_
SECTION_8_MY_

S
_ACES
INGREDIENTS
TIVE_IMPACT
GREDIENTS
A_EXPERIENCE
AR
AMILIES

ONE OF US

Foreword by JOAN ROCA

In the vibrant heart of Lima, the cradle of Peruvian gastronomy, there's a magical place called "Mayta". This restaurant is a spot where flavours intertwine with passion and creativity, and its chef, Jaime Pesaque, is the architect of this unique culinary experience.

I'm very lucky to be able to travel the world visiting restaurants. I often come across wonderful stories that chefs who passed through our house have shared with us. Likewise, I've experienced extraordinary moments of great joy by the young people from different parts of the world who have come to Girona looking for training and inspiration, and who would also end up leaving their mark at El Celler de Can Roca.

It's an honour for me to contribute to this book written by Jaime, a talented chef that I had the pleasure of meeting a few years ago at our place. From the word go, it was clear that Jaime had a passion for gastronomy and a tireless desire to explore new culinary frontiers. He joined our team, shared the values of our great family and took them with him; that's why we consider him one of ours.

Jaime is recognised as one of the most prominent and influential chefs in Latin America. His work at Mayta has been fundamental in projecting an exceptional image of Peruvian gastronomy in the world. Along with Gastón Acurio and Virgilio Martínez, he has elevated Peruvian culture and products to the top, proudly displaying the diversity and excellence of his cuisine.

This book serves as a window to Jaime's creative process, where he shares his recipes, his techniques and his culinary experiences. Through its pages, the book invites us to explore the fascinating world of Peruvian cuisine.

Jaime has mapped an exciting path through the secrets and mysteries hidden in the Andes, the Amazon and the Pacific, infinite spaces from which the raw materials for his restaurant are sourced. The prodigious work carried out with the unique paiche or pirarucú fish, the Arapaima gigas, is remarkable. For a European with lazy Mediterranean rivers, it's almost impossible to imagine a river fish three metres long and weighing around 200 kilograms, capable of breathing out of water and feeding on the vegetation that grows on the banks.

Jaime takes advantage of absolutely everything, even more so than with a pig, as the scales are used for jewellery and its skin for wallets. In Mayta, the skin is dehydrated and transformed into tableware, just like its entire skeleton. Its raspy bony tongue stays in the kitchen, but it isn't cooked, rather it's used to grate, much the same way that some use it to sand wood.

Personally, it's as equally amazing and impressive to take in any part of the paiche fish that my friend Jaime Pesaque has prepared as it is to see the dishes arrive plated atop the fish's skull or other part of the skeleton. It's truly extraordinary!

I greatly appreciate his philosophy of making use of every bit of any product that comes into his kitchen. At El Celler we share this idea of maximum benefit and minimum waste. It's something we learnt from our parents, and that we learned again in our travels through the Amazon and we're going to trumpet throughout the world the idea that kitchens, professional or domestic, return to the circular economy. We must try to restore everything that we have taken excessively from Tierra Noble, our Noble Land. Certainly, Tierra Noble is a beautiful concept that's entirely applicable to Mayta, a restaurant that works diligently for sustainability, biodiversity and respect for its cultures.

Jaime Pesaque is a member of that group of Peruvian chefs who have taught, educated and given so much to the world, be it products, techniques, ways of living, exploring, fusing and communicating. Peru, with its biodiversity, with all its microclimates, with its cultural realities, is an example for the planet.

We must celebrate once again that a great Peruvian chef has presented us such a valuable book that, I'm sure, will become an essential reference. Congratulations on the great work and thank you very much for the gift!

MERCADO

MAYTA MEANS '
IN THE AYMARA

AN ODE TO THE

ERRA NOBLE'
ANGUAGE.

OBLE LAND.

SECTION_1_INTR

S

JAIME PESAQUE, MY LIFE

My story, like that of many Peruvians, begins on the boats that transported people of diverse nationalities across oceans to start afresh. Migration is a foundation of Peru's melting pot and, in my family's case, my great-grandparents came from the Netherlands and Greece, leaving their homelands to begin new lives. My maternal *tatarabuelo* Guillermo Roose Campos came from the Netherlands, but curiously there was never much connection in my family with that food culture.

I was born in Lima's San Isidro district and raised in various *limeño* neighbourhoods such as Monterrico, Miraflores and La Molina. My mother Patricia Roose, from the Dutch side of the family, owned a textiles factory that knitted sweaters for North American brands, while my father Raúl Otero ran a factory producing juices and flours.

My family is large, and I have siblings from both sides of my parents. As youngsters we'd all eat together because gathering at the dining table is an integral part of Peruvian culture. On Sundays, we'd do a big shop then prepare breakfast together, cooking scrambled eggs with huachana sausage and pork ribs, and squeezing fruit for fresh juices.

I was quite the glutton as a kid. I always enjoyed eating – everything. I'd wake up and my first question would be what we'd have for lunch, and if I didn't like what was on the 'menu', I'd plan my day accordingly. The *chifa* (Chinese-Peruvian) spot on the corner was a favourite for noodles with wontons and rice, a classic, or *chifa aeropuerto* made with chicken, noodles and ginger. I'd often have a stew at school then get home at 3:30 pm and have a second lunch. I'd also go to Guillermo and Lucha's house, my grandparents, whose lives did revolve around food. The whole family, 40 of us with cousins, would go there every Monday between 6pm and 8.30pm for an early supper of sandwiches, ham, cheese and fruit. I spent a lot of time at my grandparent's house growing up, studying, cooking, eating. Obviously I was pretty chubby.

At home we'd often eat roast chicken and *aji de gallina*, Peruvian comfort food made with chicken swimming in a creamy yellow chilli pepper sauce. But the three traditional dishes our family ate on a weekly basis were *ají de atun* that replaced hen with tuna; *olluquito con carne*, made with the sliced Andean tuber and mixed and again, yellow chilli pepper. There was no escaping the family dinner to eat somewhere else; that was non-negotiable.

Eating has always been a pleasure for me and I was a gannet. When I was 12, I started watching cooking shows, not normal behaviour for a kid that age back then. In the last few years of high school, I told my parents I was interested in cooking. There weren't many opportunities to do so at the time, but they encouraged me anyway.

I took some courses, my mum getting permission for me to miss school for one week at a time; it was me and 35 older ladies taking classes with a French chef. When I was 15, I started to prepare 'meals', following recipes on weekends. After graduating high school, I undertook work experience for a summer at Al Fresco, then went to Lima's Cordon Bleu.

One great opportunity was working towards a Masters' degree in cuisine at the Instituto Culinario Italiano (ICIF) in Asti, because the school helped organise *stages* in interesting restaurants such as El Cellar de Can Roca. I lived between Spain and Italy for two years.

I was 24 when I returned to Lima and, at that time, an opportunity arose to open my own restaurant. I had just come back from Europe and was finding myself as a Peruvian chef as well as learning how to be a leader and a professional. So I started travelling around Peru – and became inspired by our diverse pantry that traverses the Amazon, the Andes and the Pacific.

When the opportunity to take over as chef at Al Grano in Lima appeared, I seized it. Up until that point, I'd been a line cook as well as second in command, but now I would be in charge of the whole kitchen as chef de cuisine serving contemporary cuisine and specialising in rice dishes such as risotto, paella and creamy *meloso* rice. I worked there for three years, when suddenly, the dream of opening my own restaurant took a step closer to reality. I undertook some more stages at El Cellar de Can Roca with Joan Roca, returned once again to Lima, and opened Mayta at the end of 2008.

In 2023, Mayta celebrated its 15th anniversary. While we have been listed in rankings and won awards throughout the years, it hasn't always been an easy ride. Bankruptcy, not just once but five times, unable to pay bills, moving premises, almost giving up... This is my story about Mayta.

MY PERU

Peru is a generous and noble land in terms of its culture and diverse and abundant pantry, so my decision to train as a cook was an easy one.

When I was younger, my family would go on vacation to Cajamarca, a northern city in the highlands found at 2,750 metres above sea level, and to Cusco, an elevated city located at 3,399 metres in the Andes that used to be the capital and administrative centre of the Inca civilisation at the start of the 15th and 16th centuries. We'd also go to Pucusana and Naplo in the summer, small fishing towns on the Pacific coast located a 90-minute drive south of Lima, and I'd while away a few hours as a kid trying to catch something with a homemade line. I've long had the bug to travel around my homeland, and beyond, because exploring means learning, seeing, smelling, touching – it nourishes my creativity and cooking.

After working in an array of Michelin-starred restaurants for two years in Italy and Spain, I came back to Peru in 2003 and found that Lima had become a place where I could enjoy and learn about French, Spanish and Italian cuisines – but curiously, we barely recognised our own Peruvian potential. Chef Gastón Acurio was just starting to convert his French restaurant into a Peruvian one, while a young Pedro Miguel Schiaffano was beginning to discover the Amazon's bounty. Putting Peru on the map as a very tasty country was a plan that lay ahead for us all – and that was very motivating.

Peru is home to 84 of the world's 104 life zones, while 28 of 32 climates shine, blow, rain and snow upon us. If you drive in a car for two hours in any direction, you'll quickly be at a new elevation where an array of ingredients are cultivated. As a cook, it's very inspiring.

Before opening Mayta in 2008, I started to travel around the country for inspiration such as the north to sample traditional northern food such as grouper ceviche and duck rice, as well as to Cusco for corn and cheese. The mountains are so beautiful, as are the communities who have made their home there for centuries, bestowing their folklore and gratitude upon the land. When they sow and harvest, when they make their pachamanca [dishes stone-baked in the earth] and huatias [a single-use mud-brick oven] – it's beautiful. I love the aromas of paico and muña, especially just after it has rained, when the mountains come alive with their perfumes.

The Amazon continues to have a huge impact on me. The jungle is a world apart, it's so unique that every time I go there I discover something 'new' such as arazá fruit or breadfruit. The market in Iquitos is a never-ending labyrinth flourishing with fruits such as macambo and copuazú, beans, freshwater fish such as carachama and gamitana, tiny vibrant-coloured chilli peppers and manioc. The sticky climates, sizzling temperatures, the amplified colours, warm and friendly people, the nocturnal sounds hissing and humming: it's the epitome of diversity. I find the Amazonian world to be very inspiring. It's a parallel world that unites Latin America.

I'm proud to be Peruvian and proud of Peru. I owe a lot to my country and my mission is to export our culture through gastronomy. I think of every restaurant I open as a modest embassy; besides Mayta, my group includes Sapiens, 500 Grados and Mad in Lima as well as others in Europe. I have to represent Peru.

Everything I do in the kitchen and in my life, is a tribute to Peru, my way of giving thanks to my country for showing me how to become an artisan of my trade. That's why I decided to give Mayta a Peruvian name: it means 'noble land' in Aymara, one of 48 Indigenous languages spoken in Peru.

MY LIMA

Growing up next to the Pacific Ocean is a privilege. The fact that it's a city in perpetual motion is what I love the most about Lima.

WLima is the place where I was born and grew up, where I got an education, made friends and met long-standing colleagues, where I met my wife, Francesca de Orbegoso, the place we got married. I've lived in several *limeño* neighbourhoods including Monterrico, Miraflores and La Molina, and today Francesca and I live with our three daughters in San Isidro, a block from Miraflores.

I'm fascinated by Lima's jutting cliffs and the movements of the waves. The very geography opens my mind and makes me think every day, how lucky we are to live next to this ever-changing deep blue sea that swirls between grey, greens and turquoise hues. Breathing in salty sea air is a truly unique wake-up call. Being able to see Barranco and Miraflores, either from the shore or from the cliffs above, looking down at the panorama of bobbing fishing boats whose hauls feed us all, tenacious surfers and the distant horizon, is breathtaking. In summer, when the clouds lift and the sky is clear blue, Lima is truly a work of art.

When I was younger, I used to go bodyboarding with a friend, riding tubes early in the morning or later in the afternoon. It's a way of escaping this marvellous yet chaotic city, its narrow streets and blaring buses. Once a week, two or three cooks walk down to the beach to gather algae and stones, taking little pieces of the ocean back to the restaurant so that our guests can also experience this life.

Lima is a cultural melting pot. A lot of people, in particular from the mountain regions, have migrated to the capital. Many members of Mayta's family moved from Cusco, Huancayo and Ayacucho for work. One of the reasons why Peru has so many hard-working and talented cooks is because we love to prepare food at home and share our different cultures at the restaurant.

Thanks to this melting pot, the food scene is incredibly diverse. From a young age I would go and eat for less than a dollar, lunching on ceviche, rice, noodles, wontons and pork sandwiches. Eating in Lima is also a luxury.

For me, my city means opportunity and it gives me the space I need to share my voice.

LIMA IS A CULTU
MELTING POT

AL

CURVA
CURVA

DESPACIO
CURVA
CURVA
DESPACIO

CO GNB
WESTIN

MY MAYTA 1.0

The opportunity to open my first restaurant was rather spontaneous and while the first 12 months went well, the intervening years were rather more complicated and I went bankrupt not once but five times.

I returned from Europe to Lima to obtain a new visa so as to go back to Italy and during the interim, a conversation began about heading my own establishment. Thinking 'this might not happen twice in my life', I decided to run with it.

I think the usual way to go about setting up a restaurant would be to draw up a business plan: hire an architect, consider the decor and design, the kitchen and so on. The restaurant didn't have a name but once I started travelling around Peru – and fell in love with my country's bountiful pantry – I knew its moniker had to be a tribute to my land, tierra noble, or Mayta in the Aymara indigenous language.

I'd gone to Europe when I was young to further my culinary education. After two years in Italy and Spain, I returned home with fresh eyes and a newfound connection between ingredients and me as a chef. Basically, I'd grown up.

Mayta, tierra noble, opened in 2008 and the menu encompassed traditional Peruvian dishes with contemporary twists that meant applying culinary techniques I'd acquired abroad. The first year was fantastic, but the next six were difficult.

The restaurant's location, on a busy street with a lot of traffic in Miraflores, wasn't the best, plus it didn't have the most welcoming of entrances. The original building was rather austere, a house that we simply dressed up to look like a restaurant. I soon realised a dining establishment needed to transport you from your home and offer an experience, allowing you to breathe in different airs and visually appreciate something novel. We had merely remodelled a house, rather than created a place to dine at, and the façade betrayed that.

As for the menu, my personal twists on traditional dishes weren't embraced by diners; we didn't understand the public but they also didn't understand us. Dishes included risotto de chupe de camarones from Arequipa, a soup that I converted into a dry soup or risotto that was both radical and strange, a twist too far. Diners didn't get the broth's lack of liquid. Then there was arroz con pato, a traditional rice dish from Piura and Chiclayo in the north. We served up the whole duck on top of the rice in the pan and diners also found that to be too weird and modern for the time.

While Mayta 2.0's cocktail bar today has a strong emphasis on pisco, at Mayta 1.0 we had a chilcano bar – chilcano being a popular traditional concoction made with pisco and ginger ale served in a highball glass – where we prepared more than 100 macerations in house. Diners loved MaracuMango; that was one of the original Mayta's success stories.

There was also the rather vertiginous learning curve of becoming a businessman, taking on the administrative side which I knew nothing about and had to learn from the word go. In the first year, I went bankrupt and quickly had to start looking for ways out, seeking new opportunities to be able to continue running Mayta.

I sold my car, took on extra jobs and borrowed money from my family, but at the end of the day, I couldn't see myself being anywhere else but at Mayta. Not cooking in a luxury hotel or selling ideas that I'd never get to fully develop or see come to fruition at another restaurant.

Things were so difficult at one point that there was barely any wine left in the cellar. But there was a shop on the corner, and when a table wanted a bottle of something – and the sale was guaranteed – a waiter would go out for three reds, usually paying for them with his own credit card. The table would buy one at a totally extortionate price, but that would pay the waiter's salary for the month. I think back to that time and laugh out loud now but to be honest, I'm grateful for those moments because they helped me grow. They also helped me realise I had to overcome this whole situation.

The first year of Mayta basically coincided with Francesca and I getting married as well as the birth of our eldest daughter. Fran injected a lot of positivity when times were hard, while my parents – both very hard workers who led successful businesses and worked almost every waking hour – had set me the example of never giving up. I understood that I needed to drive the business forward, not give up on my dream and to continue believing in myself, because it was now my turn to set an example to my daughter.

Some nights I cried, trying not to wake Fran with my sobbing, because I hadn't got any money for the next day. It was just awful and while I ate a lot of shit during that time, I later realised it hadn't tasted so bad. I'm thankful for those hard times today, because they gave me a thicker skin.

Take the pandemic in 2020. A lot of colleagues were worried because they didn't know how to manage the continually unravelling situation. But I knew how to take decisions, be creative and not stress out. That's when Mad Burger came to be, the first brand in Lima born out of necessity during the pandemic – and there are now four storefronts with a fifth due to open in Miami. I had trained myself to take tough decisions and we were able to share that experience. Mayta's chefs were suddenly flipping burgers, waitstaff stuffing paper bags with fries and onion rings, but we continued together as a team. That's the spirit of Mayta, applied to Mad Burger, everyone working together despite being totally different concepts.

In around 2010, Gastón Acurio started exporting the concept of Peruvian cuisine, so I started undertaking consulting jobs and those helped plug the gap in my negative finances.

For a decade, Mayta basically served up the same menu out of that Miraflores establishment when an issue with the local council arose. I didn't make a dramatic or fast decision but I had been feeling for a long time that the restaurant needed a different location. The council's new norm required us to build our own car park, which would basically take up a huge chunk of the restaurant that was only able to accommodate 28 guests and would more than halve that – and so I decided to move.

In the last 18 months of Mayta 1.0, I was already drawing up the plans for my second restaurant. A casual eatery, 500 Grados was in the pipeline but it was hard to find a suitable storefront: it ended up taking a year. Just 24 hours after I decided Mayta needed to start afresh, a new space miraculously opened up. It was a clear message that I had to move on – and drive forward.

MATACUY

MY MAYTA 2.0

The lofty swinging front door you walk through to enter Mayta creates a warm yet impressive welcome. Still, it's the bar and copper alembic that will likely turn your attention to choosing an apéretif. High ceilings are conducive for planting a hanging garden including fan palms, Delta maidenhair and elkhorn ferns, establishing a connection with nature. To the left of the bar is the main salon and the kitchen. Peep through the open kitchen window and you'll see me or chefs Santiago, Felipe or Richard finishing dishes. To the right of the bar, a little orange light slices through window panes framed by foliage, warming up the secondary dining area. My favourite spot (besides in the kitchen) is perched at the bar sipping coffee while chatting with the bar team.

Moving premises to a more dynamic part of Miraflores meant it was time to start cooking up my dreams for real.

When we took over a property on an iconic corner of Avenida La Mar, we completely remodelled the space: it was a chance to strengthen and energise Mayta in every way possible, from the menu to hiring a team to cook every day, a team that would become family, and start afresh. The ensuing work that followed focused on details from cutlery and dishware to ingredients sourced from all over Peru, and everything was created by artisans. It was the opportunity to set up a new cultural embassy, populate it with highly skilled culinary ambassadors, and share Peru's heritage through gastronomy. In December 2018, Mayta 2.0 was born.

The food itself took on a new lease of life. Gone were the traditional dishes with those contemporary twists such as the *risotto de chupe de camarones* that had confused diners. I began devising a precise tasting menu born simply out of creativity. Continually inspired by Peru's pantry, it's impossible to find the link to the second version of Mayta with the traditions of the first restaurant, and while it might transport you to a region, it won't lead you to a specific dish. Mayta the Second bears its own identity.

Sharing our interpretation of Peruvian identity is crucial and so is running a sustainable kitchen. The tasting menu changes according to ingredient availability and over the course of a year, it is totally revamped three times.

My inspiration for the 11-course EXPERIENCIA MAYTA MENU starts in Yachay, an expedition to Peru's fertile desert three hours south of Lima, where dunes meet the ocean. It's important to take a breath of fresh air from the restaurant and that's where the menu's story begins.

We have a privileged pantry thanks to the sierras, the jungle and the ocean and rivers. We don't try to cook cleverly creative dishes but rather, prepare handcrafted ones conveying origin and respect for the products. I love to include lots of outlines so guests can also tap into their own creativity and reach their own conclusion. It's a special journey.

The menu isn't heavy going because we want you to savour it and digest comfortably. We play around with vegetables and herbs as well as tubers; there are just two meat proteins – alpaca and beef ribs from Oxapampa – then fish and seafood.

There's also an à la carte option and while I no longer serve a whole duck in the pan, *arroz con pato* still forms part of the menu, taking a heart-warming approach to comfort food.

I was able to take my time with this reconstruction, giving thought to the process and digging deeper when it came to sharing Peruvian identity and creating a timeless space at Mayta 2.0. It was important to use natural tones that noble raw materials such as cachimbo timber and stone afford in the décor. The dining tables, for example, were handcrafted from river rocks sourced from near the Huancavelica River (*huanca* means stone in Quechua). Handmade porcelain tiles line the floor, while wood rolls out in furniture design. A great spot to start the evening is on a comfy leather stool at the bar; the counter is also made from cachimbo. Red clay and wooden elements are incorporated into the walls to warm up the ambience, while more fern greenery runs the length of the windows. I made the most of the elevated ceilings for the hanging garden that also created practical storage space in lofty shelves.

Every piece of ceramic dishware or glassware was bespoke designed for Mayta, and we also repurpose carachama fish skeletons, dehydrating them in the oven, polish moro crab shells and dry cacao pods to create other unique recipients.

Mayta is an extension of me, and the vehicle through which I explore my curiosity for Peru. And with the Mayta family, we push our kitchen and drinks creativity as a way of honouring Peru's gastronomic heritage, while and hoping to inspire our guests' curiosity as well.

SECTION_2_MY_

_ACES

Peru is one of the world's 17 most biodiverse countries, home to an incredible 84 of the world's 103 ecosystems as well as 28 of the 32 climates that exist on planet Earth. In this chapter, I'd like to share six regions that I frequent, from the capital where I was born and raised to the Amazon and its complex water network as well as Yachay, our organic garden.

Iquitos is the gateway city to the Amazon, a buzzy port city thanks to its commercial activities and flying insects, and it offers a marvellous snapshot of a populated corner of the world's largest tropical rainforest.

Located on the Itaya River, Iquitos boomed economically at the start of the 20th century due to a highly productive rubber industry. I find the city fascinating thanks to the chaotic Belén Market, an endless warren of passages and narrow streets whose small and diverse storefronts specialise in medicinal herbs – bark, roots and herbal elixirs are an essential part of Amazon culture and cure every ill or heartache – vegetables and prehistoric-looking fish. The market is so rich and diverse, as you walk around you might come face to face with toothy fish heads or paiche scales perfect for filing down fingernails. It's a bubble within a bubble.

The heat is always on in Iquitos and varies in intensity depending on whether it's the rainy or dry season. Hawkers ply their wares, flogging açaí juice and coconut water, or cooking up patarashca (it translates as 'wrapped up'), a grilled fish tucked inside bijao, an aromatic and tasty banana leaf with stew. Almost every dish comes wrapped in leaves, and bananas themselves are very versatile, baked in embers or fried depending on how ripe they are.

More than 1,100 tributaries flow through the Amazon basin, and Iquitos is the connecting point that unveils the rainforest through its watery passages. You can smell life through humidity; the earth is always damp. Water levels depend on the season, although hard drought tends to occur between June and September, Lima's winter. Houses are built on stilts and raised off the ground to prevent flooding when the crest of the river rises.

I travel here with chef Santiago to visit the Yanayacu fishing community. It takes several hours to reach this destination travelling by canoe. An electric generator hums away in the village, a token connection to civilisation but beyond that, the way they live – forging an existence or at best, a living, from hunting, fishing and agriculture – you can either interpret it as precarious or a sanctuary.

Granted permission from the apu, the head of the community, to pitch up our tents in a communal space, the strident sounds of the jungle can be both terrifying and relaxing. Birds, insects, crickets, all kinds of animals are out there chirping, singing, buzzing and whistling, and this chatter makes it clear that the jungle is truly alive. Everyone wakes up early with the first rays of sun, if not before. And when it's the designated fishing season, the fishermen's association works from dawn until dusk, descaling paiche and salting it.

The community leads by democracy: when we ask to go fishing, they vote on it as all decisions are made collectively. Its members are also easily adaptable: searching for a little dry firewood or fallen bark leads them to a palm tree from which they gather some fruit. Everything grows freely, even if they keep chickens. Between so few people, trust is paramount.

They are also the most hospitable people: together we eat fish caught from the river, or freshly hunted meat as well as bananas and yucca, and every other day, rice. There's a seemingly endless supply of fish, meat, birds and plants as well as bananas and pineapples within easy grabbing distance. Every home's garden cultivates ají charapita chilli pepper, coconut and sacha culantro, the most commonly used ingredients when it comes to cooking daily. The Amazon pantry knows no bounds.

THE ANDES

What can I say about The Andes? The mountains are a Peruvian treasure trove.

Around 20 ranges make up the rocky backbone of South America, and there are almost 21,500 named mountains in Peru. Their slopes and valleys can be both fertile and hostile, hospitable for the hundreds of communities who have lived here for centuries yet unfriendly to the outsider who can find it difficult to simply breathe at two, three or four thousand metres above sea level.

The Andes slide between valleys and peaks, snowmelt feeding rivers and waterfalls, which in turn nourish the highlands.

Thousands of varieties of potatoes and tubers that bear dazzling pigmentation – magenta, indigo, saffron – reliably grow in unusual shapes, taking on the appearance of flora or animals. Hundreds of chilli peppers with a little or a lot of bite, another vibrant palette into which an artist would love to dip their brush.

But beyond a plentiful pantry that springs out from one of the world's most astounding topographies, it's the Andean people who nurture the land and captivate me with their charm. We work with corn farmers in the Huancayo area, located at more than 3,300 metres above sea level, and it is truly remarkable how they convert stoney hillsides into flourishing farmland that successfully cultivates large-kernel corn. This is yet another Andean crop that runs the gamut of the pigmentation palette with striking blue, red and purple hues (the latter's kernels are used to make chicha morada, a favourite Peruvian soft drink). These farmers are experts in their field, depending solely on rainfall and the fertile yet hostile land to raise beautiful, robust ears.

The Andes truly is the manifestation of abundance. Tunta, a potato that is dried at high altitudes during the Andean 'ice age' between June and August, comes from Puno, as does the cushuro cyanobacteria that's gathered from the region's freezing elevated lakes. Then, edible flowers are cultivated at lower levels. Daisies, for example, come from Acobamba Valley, where a favourable geography protects the land from frost and radically contrasts with the irregular peaks in Puno. These are just some of the treasures we have discovered in the Andes and there are surely many to discover.

BODEGA SAN NICOLÁS PISCO 1615

A sea of green vine leaves shudder on the ocean breeze, lapping at the blue sky. At their roots, a sandy whirling dervish kicks up a fuss. On a clear day, the Pacific twinkles in the distance. When a desert vineyard meets a coastal desert, there's just one word to describe it: contrasting. This is the place we chose to start making the family pisco.

My brother Raúl cultivates four varieties of pisco grapes in this peculiar and very special terroir, located just 10 kilometres from the Pacific Ocean. Not only is there coastal influence but it's also a stone's throw from the bountiful Paracas natural reserve in the district of Pisco. Sandy and saline soils merge to create a curiously fertile terroir; a short drive from the distillery you can suddenly be traversing Peru's answer to the Sahara. Sand dunes shift with the Pacific air currents; the apparently arid topography makes it seem impossible that waves are beating out their rhythm so close by, or that agriculture is as productive as it is.

When we were growing up, Dad would buy bottles of pisco and we young people enjoyed making and drinking chilcanos. It was a time when pisco was being rediscovered by a new generation: us. A family friend had founded the brand in 2006; that was Bodega San Nicolás Pisco 1615's first chapter. Then, in 2011 the opportunity to put our own distinctive mark on the spirit came to light – and we seized it.

We focus on cultivating the Quebranta, Torrontel, Italia and Albilla varieties, which are trained on a vine arbour system. Following the harvest, the grapes are fermented to make wine that in turn is distilled to make Peru's national spirit.

Our mission as a bodega and distillery is to reintroduce pisco to the world, create the second wave, kickstart a renaissance if you like. That's why we have gone back to pisco's roots – to a noble land of contrast, where the coastal desert merges with a desert vineyard – to tell the story of our pisco, Bodega San Nicolás Pisco 1615.

LIMA'S COAST

Lima is such a beautiful city. Located on the Pacific coast, shielded by a protective cliff, it boasts a climate that's neither too cold nor too hot. Just perfect. It's a little grey, obviously, because of the fog. But the sky clears in the summer and our capital flourishes even more, fiery Royal poinciana blossom, shocking pink bougainvillaea and cooing doves lifting the mood. Step up from the beach to the cliffs and there are incredible views looking out over the waves, surfers and fishing boats bobbing on the horizon.

The coast goes on and on, north towards Pirua and south toward Arequipa, merging with a fertile desert where asparagus, citrus fruits, apples, pecans, almonds, papayas, chilli peppers and corn thrive. This deceptively barren-looking land merges with the sea, and a bit further south we have a privileged marine pantry to dip into. Scallops, clams, sea snails, fish such as chita (Anisotremus scapularis), sea bass and sole, as well as octopus and squid.

I think we limeños are very kind and hardworking people, always happy to help. Good people with good hearts who try to be proactive and do things well. The outsider's perspective is that we are rather creative, let's say, when it comes to inventing jobs. It's a Lima trait, but also a Latin American one, right? We are all a jack of all trades. And despite Peru's economic difficulties, we always try to have a good time – and always try to eat well.

If there is one thing that unites us (in addition to football) across the entire social spectrum, it's food. Wealthier limeños can prepare lobster causas while others on lower income might use canned tuna. But at the end of the day, both are united by gastronomy, by food, by our very culture. And that's what makes us proud, and unites us.

PARACAS NATIONAL RESERVE

Few places on the Peruvian coast are as unique as the Paracas Peninsula or as topographically and archaeologically relevant. Our coastline is linear, creating a naturally sheltered bay that's a treasure for mariculture. Thanks to its biodiversity – from plankton to Humboldt penguins – Paracas is also a protected national reserve.

One of eight districts in the province of Ica, 10 million years ago the saffron-coloured peninsular was an island. But the volcanic eruptions caused by the Nazca tectonic plates – the ones whose sporadic shakes keep us dancing on our toes – pushed the land up, creating a rocky kind of bridge made of pink granodiorite and magma.

Inhabited by the prehistoric Paracas civilisation around 800 BCE – who are thought to have depicted the Candelabra geoglyph, although other wilder theories abound – today the low cliffs and sandy dunes in this low-profile spot are loved by those in the know for the plentiful wildlife on Ballestas Islands and the remarkable red sands of Playa Roja. A four-hour drive south of Lima, the topography and open spaces are a breath of fresh air from the capital.

The water is a beautiful green because it is loaded with plankton, which comes in from the south on the Humboldt Current. The current collides with the peninsula, forming a natural whirlpool that mixes the Pacific waters with the bay's. It's a particular phenomenon that occurs in just two or three places along our coast, ensuring calm waters and gentle waves. If you looked at droplets under a microscope, you'd see an incredible number of things moving and swimming. It's full of life.

These tasty plankton allows molluscs such as razor clams and scallops, and fish such as anchovies to feed, which in turn are fodder for the moro crab. The sandier the seabed, the happier the mollusc.

This blue-hued moro crab is, in fact, a predator and sworn enemy of Luis Verue, our shellfish farmer who says the moro can crack open and devour 60 scallops a day with its large claws.

The Paracas Bay is an underwater diner, filled with riches and no creature has to really work hard for its supper. The food chain is lengthy – and we also form part of it. (We appreciate the moro for its special flavour that a mollusc-intense diet gives it.)

It's a dream scenario for a cook to have an organic garden at their fingertips, one where dreams can be sown then later harvested.

The absolute beauty of having our own little farm is choosing what we would like to pluck from the earth or pick from a bush in three or four months, in summer or autumn: Yachay is the nucleus from which we design EXPERIENCIA MAYTA MENU.

Farmer Carlos Chipana takes care of this beautiful space every single day, sowing seeds, fertilising seedlings, watering herbs and vegetables, rotating products, picking them when they are ready. It's a craft and he is the artisan who cultivates with his own hands.

The Yachay fruit and vegetable garden is the sister of the pisco grape vineyards at Bodega San Nicolás Pisco 1615 in Ica. Both projects share the land, which is about 240 kilometres south of Lima and a short drive from Paracas Bay. This is Peru's coastal desert, a surprisingly fertile place whose soil is influenced by the Pacific Ocean of the past as well as its cooling maritime breezes of the present day.

Yachay connects those of us in the kitchen to our noble land in a profound way. It guides us through seasonality and temporality, success and failure, and the ability to choose. It can also be frustrating; not knowing how to cultivate asparagus in the early days, for example, was hugely disconcerting. Then there was the time we planted five squash seedlings and those monsters invaded the whole garden. We couldn't give them away! And there are challenges, such as losing crops to blight and pests because Yachay adheres to an organic agricultural philosophy, for example. In the beginning we didn't know which plants protected other plants and an army of ants would march through and destroy every plant in sight. Yachay is our constant teacher, and we never stop learning.

Spending time there during the pandemic – when we couldn't open the restaurant – was an absolute blessing. The Mayta family went there frequently, learning about herbs, legumes, vegetables and fruit, and how to make compost and humus with Carlos. A true gift.

With 36 different crops growing on average at any one time, there is always a reason to put your hands in the earth. There are always two or three types of lettuce and chilli peppers on the go. Then there are root vegetables such as sweet potato, carrots, cassavas and potatoes; aromatic herbs such as muña, chincho and basil; stalky greens such as broccoli; loche squash, chard, leeks, endives, and many members of the allium family. In summer, the creepers are dripping with blackberries and raspberries, while we are almost drowning in tomatoes, they do so well. Of course, we make use of everything because, through our frustrations, we now understand the sacrifices made when it comes to cultivating those tomatoes as well as the cost of buying a jar of sauce. We have learned a true appreciation for what's valuable.

Yachay is a cook's dream. It inspires us, motivates us, challenges us and can also frustrate us. It's where Mayta's philosophy is born.

SECTION_3_MY_

GREDIENTS

While we work with more than 100 ingredients sourced from all over Peru, in this chapter I'd like to share five notable products that are close to my heart: scallops gathered from a treasured Pacific bay, cacao and river fish from the Amazon basin, and oca and cushuro from the Andes. And in the next chapter, I will highlight an additional 26 ingredients that are core to the Experiencia Mayta Menu.

CACAO

Now, I want to share a different perspective of the Amazon with you. Normally we think of tributaries and rainforest in Peru's largest ecoregion, and that is what cacao requires, plenty of precipitation and high temperatures.

Cultivated in Peru since pre-Columbian times, three of the world's 10 Theobroma cacao varieties are cultivated in our country: Forastero amazónico, which accounts for the majority grown on farms, Criollo and Trinitario, the latter a hybrid of the aforementioned varieties.

Peru is one of the top-10 cacao producers in the world, its seeds or beans usually cultivated by small producers who own two or fewer hectares of plantation land.

Cacao requires high temperatures, plenty of rainfall and only grows between 20 degrees north and south of the equator. It also loves the shade of the towering rainforest canopy.

This bean's recent history is fascinating: it was introduced as a substitute product to farmers, enabling those families affected by drug trafficking to replace coca leaf plantations with cacao. It adapted well, producing high-quality beans, and that paid off: between the years 2000 and 2021, exports rose 15-fold, according to the Observatory of Economic Complexity, thanks to the rising demand for bean-to-bar products.

A noble shrub, a tiny pod emerges from every cream-coloured blossom, and it's vital that farmers prune to improve concentration and ensure maximum vigour, just like Vitis vinifera grapes.

We source golden chuncho cacao pods from farmers in the San Martín department in the province of Tarapoto, in the western region of the Amazon basin close to the Huallaga River.

A member of the native Forastero family, the chuncho variety loves the inclined slopes and extreme heat the mountains located in the middle of the jungle offer.

Notable flavours include citrus and floral notes as well as unripe banana and notes.

Cacao is a dreamy ingredient to create with as it's so versatile. We use the pod's husk, beans, the mucilage and nibs as well as the main by-product of chocolate.

We especially love the sweet and aromatic pulp that covers the beans, using this mucilage to make clouds and sorbets. Reducing it creates an aromatic and citric honey with floral aromas and its beautiful cacao notes. We use that honey in sorbet.

By taking the pod's vein, to which the seeds were connected, and dehydrating it, we make an infusion along with the husk.

As for the chocolate itself, we use it in ganaches and mousses that rotate in the MUCILAGOS dessert course.

D

CONCHAS

In Chapter 2, I mentioned the enormous benefits of the Humboldt Current on the wide biodiversity of the Paracas Bay, especially its abundance of shellfish, but for me the concha or scallop stands out.

What I love about this marine bivalve mollusk is its sweet flavour combined with saline notes. When they are extremely fresh, conchas are fleshy and firm; note that these bivalves are hermaphrodites.

Their flavour comes from a plankton-heavy diet, riches carried in on the Humboldt Current-driven tides in these waters.

In this bay, shellfish breed of their own accord in natural sandbanks, but are also cultivated by breeders who take advantage of this precious resource. Concha 'seeds' are often transported from northern Peru then 'sown' in carefully constructed aquatic farms.

Mayta works with breeder Luis Vereu, whose team raise and harvest these bivalves by hand across 10 hectares of sea bed. It's an arduous and highly artisanal way of doing things: starting very early in the morning, with a tube of oxygen clenched between their lips, masked divers free swim down to a depth of between three and five metres – the sea bed here doesn't go much deeper than that – and gather conchas by hand, placing them into a long cylindrical net known as a linterna.

The waters maintain a stable temperature as there are few big waves and in winter it starts at 20°C: the bay acts like a gigantic aquarium, the ideal dining room for other marine bivalve molluscus including the Pacific razor clam and clams.

When they see divers approaching, the conchas get a little scared and 'run off', flapping and leaping through the transparent green depths. But, because they eventually hit a wall, they can't actually escape. Luis says it's a bit like raising chickens, only at the bottom of the sea, and free-range chickens at that, given that the conchas have a totally organic diet.

While there's little more delicious than just-opened conchas and dripping a little fresh lime juice into the soft body protected by the ribbed hinged shell, we dehydrate them in the kitchen.

First, we cure the coral with a salt and sugar mixture for an hour and then we dehydrate in the sun before adding it to PARACAS, the second course in the EXPERIENCIA MAYTA MENU.

CUSHURO

From the opposite side of the Andean spectrum to the oca, this ingredient is a cyanobacteria that thrives in the freezing waters of elevated lakes in the mountains.

Nostoc sphaericum, better known as cushuro, is commonly referred to as a Andean algae, although it is actually a cyanobacteria that grows wild in the lakes.

These small spheres vary in colour between a metallic green and earthy dark brown and are highly nutritious, boasting high quantities of calcium and iron as well as a range of B vitamins.

Cushuro also goes by the names murmunta, llullucha and llayta.

It's hard work gathering these little gelatine baubles that look similar to caviar but are larger in size and aren't always perfectly spherical in shape. First, it can be tough for humans to simply breathe at 3,000 metres or more above sea level, where they reproduce in nitrogen-dense waters. Then there are the freezing lakes: somebody has to wade in, close to the shores, and harvest them by hand using a strainer and gathering the balls into a bucket.

Regardless of the season, cushuro reproduces in both the dry and rainy seasons in the Andes.

Communities gather cushuro from the Cusco region, specifically from Moquegua and Puno, taking great care to harvest this uncultivated cyanobacteria.

The good news is that despite coming from so high and so far, cushuro is stable out of water and its natural habitat, so it reaches Mayta perfectly intact.

In the kitchen we pickle it with a traditional mixture of water, red wine, vinegar and sugar to preserve it.

We choose the prettiest baubles to finish the ALPACA course of the menu.

OCA

The next notable ingredient I want to tell you about comes from the Andes, is an important part of Andean gastronomy and comes from a 900-strong family.

An Andean crop, the oca tuber belongs to the oxalis tuberosa family and around 900 varieties are cultivated in Peru.

This underground stem tuber formed a vitally important part of the pre-Inca and Inca diet in the Andes region.

In the Quechua language it is called uqa.

It is cultivated at between 3,000 and 4,000 metres above sea level in tough terrain and requires little water.

Resistant to plagues and bugs, oca thrives at these great elevations.

Freshly-sprouting oca 'seeds' are sown ahead of the Andes' rainy season so that the seedlings will begin to flower in December, January and February. The above-ground plants are small bushes, about 20 to 30 centimetres high, and the oca tuber has an irregular, cylindrical shape with several folds.

The first couple of tubers then appear toward the end of the rainy season.

Besides the tuber itself that's hoed out of the ground, we also use its trifoliate leaves that leave a lovely acidity in the mouth, contrasting well in desserts.

The oca is also considered to be ceremonial food and is traditionally cooked in the huatia adobe brick oven and eaten during Inti Raymi festival of the sun god that is held on 24 June.

Diverse in colour, a rainbow of yellow, black or deep purple, pink and even red, strident hues that mean oca is high in antioxidants. It is also high in sugar. The yellow oca is most commonly sold in markets, given that the red and black grow at higher elevations and are therefore more difficult to transport.

Usually harvested in May and June during the dry season, the Inca used to dehydrate oca. First, they would wash then dry them well, before letting them 'sunbathe' so sugars became more concentrated.

Oca has long been used as a potato substitute and can be stored for several months at a time in straw cylinders that retain moisture well and maintain the necessary temperature.

In Mayta, we prepare oca in two ways. The first is a very light cooking point, so it's still crisp in the mouth and also makes the most of its acidity. We cook them in a base with equal proportions of white wine, water and vinegar and a little sugar. Once crispy, we then pickle them.

We also cook oca for longer periods to obtain a creamy texture that allows its sweetness to stand out. By slowly confiting them in butter for more than an hour, they become extremely soft.

PAICHE

Now I want to share the story of a legendary Amazon fish, the largest to traverse the 1,100 rivers and tributaries that weave a watery network through the world's most biodiverse rainforest.

Paiche or Arapaima gigas is the largest fish that inhabits the Amazon basin. A native to these fresh waters, it also goes by the name of pirarucu in other South American countries.

Living in small groups in medium-deep waters, it's an obligate air breather that has to regulate its oxygen levels by surfacing every 20 minutes or so.

Paiche can measure up to three metres in length, and weighs between 220 and 250 kilos.

This carnivorous predator eats small fish and crustaceans as well as plants

In Peru, there are wild paiche as well as paiche fish farms. With regard to the former, the Peruvian government allocates a fishing quota to Indigenous communities based on their human population.

We work with the Yagua ethnic group, a community of fishermen who live in Yanayacu. They fish for wild specimens in the Apayacu river between July and September, the permitted fishing season.

The name 'Yanayacu' has a special significance: in the indigenous Yagua language, Yana means black, while Yacu means water, thereby black river. Apa, meanwhile, means father, so the Apayacu River is known as Father of the Water.

Reaching this community is tricky. First, you have to reach Iquitos, gateway city to the Amazon region, then navigate down river for around six hours until you reach Yanayacu, located in the department of Loreto.

July, August and September denote the 'dry' season in the Amazon, when less water flows through the rivers and streams; regardless mosquitoes and bugs make their presence more than known. In the dry season, cochas or giant pools are created naturally and, because they can't return to deeper waters before the river dries up, adult paiches become trapped. The 23 fishermen we work with regularly visit these cochas in their territory.

It's a collaborative effort on fishing days, which tend to be hot with little precipitation. The community prepares the nets and food for the day, then searches for paiche together. After identifying an individual, fishermen approach it with handmade nets, then corner it.

A common preparation in the Amazon is conserving fish loins in salt then rolling them up and storing them until needed.

At Mayta we make full use of the whole fish. As well as the tasty belly meat to make sausages, we smoke the loin and also make ham. After thoroughly cleaning the heads, we salt them then boil them to use for stock. The bones, meanwhile, are used as models to create alternative dishware that reflects the PECES AMAZONICOS course.

-OLLUCO CONFITADO
-ALPACA COCINA
-OLLUCO MANTEQUILLA
-ALPACA SACHADA
-OLLUCO ENCURTIDO
-OLLUCO ENCURTIDO PICADO
-DEMI
-ESCABECHE
-CHIPS OLLUCO
-SUCULENTAS
-POLLO ESCABECHE

MESA 14
3.00 EXPERIENCIA YACHAY (RED)
- (EY) PAICHE* 3.00
- EY ALPACA 3.00
- (EY) YACON* 3.00
- (EY) TUMBO* 3.00
Caja : 004 - DIEGO CASTRO

SECTION_4_POS

IVE_IMPACT

Some of the challenges in the kitchen are ensuring traceability and wasting as little as possible, squeezing every last drop out of ingredients.

Total Respect For Ingredients

While I accentuate particular ingredients, such as aubergine, paiche or tumbo, the reality is that only a small portion of that product makes it onto the tasting menu. That's why an environmentally conscious approach at Mayta is essential, respecting every product and working toward having as little waste as possible.

While some fresh produce including herbs and some fruits and vegetables come from Yachay, the little organic farm where we cultivate ingredients in Ica, we also work with growers, artisanal fishermen and farmers across Peru. And in the bid to waste as little as possible, we literally squeeze every last drop from products, the juice, the skin, the seeds and pulp, just like a lemon. We dehydrate, soak, stew, press and mash, every possible part is used; for example, dried corn cobs make for excellent kindling and are used to ignite open fires at all the restaurants. We work towards zero waste at all times.

The traceable approach came organically to us, because Yachay was very much trial and error in the beginning. The labour of love and reality that is tending to land, planting seeds, transplanting seedlings, cultivating and raising healthy ingredients, harvesting them then finally cooking with them, well, it was hard.

It's an organic garden so not all the carrots are perfect or beautiful, and aubergines wildly vary in size because some flourished better than others. They'd be delivered at the restaurant and we'd ask ourselves, 'what do we do with this'? We couldn't just throw them out because they didn't meet a 'normalised' industrial standard, plus we had a special affection for that vegetable, because we'd grown it. That's when we developed a greater sensitivity and respect toward every ingredient, quickly realising that traceability was essential and not throwing anything away became part of Mayta's DNA.

We began contemplating products differently. Richard, who is head of development, only sees the benefits of an entire ingredient. With Santiago and Felipe, we analyse all the possibilities before we start to create, so as to have a long-term positive impact.

An advantage to serving an additional à la carte menu at Mayta means that unused supplies receive a new lease of life as a garnish, in restaurant dishes and in family food [staff meals]. Using all ingredients to a maximum allows us to generate a connection with guests. We share with them the carrots' origins and the reasons we select their size or shape: the small ones are for plating, while the big ones are for sautés and stock – it's important to divulge that information.

I've mentioned aubergine a few times and it really is one of the most wonderful examples of total respect in a restaurant because we simply use up everything. This spongy berry comes in three sizes, large, medium and small, and we make the most of each in different ways and for different reasons.

Using the largest samples that weigh between 400 grams and 500 grams, first we peel the skins. We make ash from the skins, which in turn is used to make a maltodextrin starch as well as an oil. We also grate the pulp and make a smooth paste that complements BERENJENAS, the third course in the tasting menu. Then, with the leftover skins, we make crispy textures.

Medium-size aubergines are less bitter in flavour, so after peeling them, we make a consommé. As for the babies, the smallest ones, we grate them for the aubergine plate. So that's where we take advantage, for example, of a product in its entirety, aubergine in its entirety.

Another star is the humble carrot. Babies are plated directly in all their naked glory complete with stems and leaves. We apply a variety of techniques to larger ones, making yoghurt, purée and creamy smoothies, also using their fresh or dry leaves, dehydrating them to make powders.

Corn is also highly versatile, which is why we devote a whole course to it, CHOCLOS. We burn the panca de choclo, or husks, to make sweet ash, and also garnish the CHOCLOS dish with corn silk. Fresh corn is used to create foam while dry corn is for tamal flour.

Then there are zapallos or squashes. There are parts of these gourds that we might not use in its entirety for the tasting menu, such as the soft innermost part, but they make the next cut in stews, sauté and curry sauce. The smallest zapallos are used as recipients while the greenest pulp is passed through a machine to make tagliatelle that forms part of the tasting menu. The oval-shaped fresh seeds are part of the finishing decorative touches. Wherever possible, we use ingredients products in their entirety.

Wellbeing In The Restaurant

More than a team, I consider Mayta to be a family, and my family has to eat really well. Because if we can't prepare a great meal made with love for our own family, then we won't be able to do it for our guests. It's one of many wellbeing goals I set for myself and the restaurant that aim to have a positive impact.

A balanced diet is important, as is the act of sitting down for a meal, and we share this simple philosophy with everyone, starting with the youngest members of the family. Dining together at a table also helps inspire performance. And while having a conversation over the two family meals, sipping the juice of the day, people will invariably chat about work but they certainly aren't executing while they're eating. Dessert forms part of the menu, because everyone deserves a sweet moment, even if it's just a little flan.

In terms of working hours, while Mayta opens every day, the family works five days on two days off on a rotational basis. Eight cooks from the 38-strong family sit down in the restaurant to enjoy the EXPERIENCIA MAYTA MENU every month; it's a virtuous and transformative circle when they see their work reflected at the table.

Mayta strives for a 100 percent approach when it comes to ingredient traceability, and when it comes to the talented Mayta family, a sustainable working environment is equally important to ensure their wellbeing and happiness in the restaurant.

SECTION_5_MAI

INGREDIENTS

While we use more than 100 ingredients soured from all over Peru at Mayta, in this chapter I want to share 26 notable products that I love to cook with, highlighting their origins, how they are cultivated, traditional cooking methods and how we use them in the kitchen.

1 Native Andean Potato

MOMENT ONE: TUBÉRCULOS

Potatoes, along with corn, are a core part of the Andean population's diet, with more than 6,000 varieties of the tubers recorded by Peru's Agricultural Innovation Institute in 2022.

At Mayta we tend to use three papas andinas or fresh native Andean potato varieties: papa negra (black); cacho de toro, also known as Puma maki or puma's paw; and yana imilla, which is round with black skin. We also use potatoes that are preserved using traditional Andean methods.

Most of what we use comes from producers in Tarma, in the Junín region, and from the Huanaco region. Geographically they are almost the same elevation, although the harvest period differs between them. Edilberto Soto is another of our key producers from the Ayacucho region.

To preserve tubers for later use, Andean communities use various ancestral conservation techniques. One is tocosh, a fermented pulp that starts with potatoes wrapped in ichu grass and left in shallow river waters for at least four months, undergoing a continual process of being washed and fermenting. They're then left to dry on the river banks for another two years. Another Andean preservation method is chuño blanco – also known as tunta in the Aymara Indigenous language and moraya in Quechua – that freeze dries potatoes by covering them with ichu grass, leaving them exposed to the sun by day and the freezing night air.

Andean potatoes are known for their vibrant flesh and tasty skin. Pigmentation varies from violet, red and yellow, as well as the textures, which can be earthy or sandy. They are irregular in shape because they have never been modified in their cultivation, and they've lots of eyes or sprouts.

Huatia is a traditional Andean cooking method that's employed during harvest time. Communities wrap up potatoes in herbs such as huacatay and chincho, build a little oven out of clay bricks, fire it up, place the potatoes inside, then collapse the oven so the potatoes are buried under the hot clay bricks.

At Mayta we thinly slice then pre-cook potatoes in clarified butter and Andean herbs, then fry them and fill them with roe, onion, tunta and yellow chilli pepper, uniting the fresh Andean potato with the preserved one in the TUBERCULOS, the first course of the EXPERIENCIA MAYTA MENU.

2 Clams, Razor clams, Stone crab & Algae

MOMENT TWO: PARACAS

CLAMS

While these bivalve molluscs dwell in natural sand banks in Paracas Bay, they are artisanally cultivated by fishermen. Clams share a common enemy with their fellow bivalves, razor clams, clams and scallops – the hefty-pincered and highly destructive stone crab. While El Niño floods and damages northern Peru, curiously the phenomenon has a positive effect in Paracas. The change in water temperature means these bivalves sense the threat that danger is on the way and are on full alert, a state that impels them to increase spawning.

These clams are meaty and saline, with a firm texture.

In Paracas, clams are eaten raw, with a touch of lime and salt and maybe chalacita, a mix of chopped red onion, culantro leaves and limo chilli pepper. At Mayta, we make a tartare with the clam's adductor muscle and emulsify the rest of the soft material such as eyes and siphons.

RAZOR CLAMS

These marine bivalve molluscs thrive on the plankton found in Paracas Bay. Farmers tend to only raise one species of bivalve, making it their speciality.

Razor clams are saline with a firm texture, and have a more delicate flavour than the other local clams. Saline when eaten raw, but exposure to heat – grilling, for example – brings out their sweet notes.

Razor clams have long been consumed in the Americas, well before Spanish colonisation, but they have never been traditionally consumed in Peru's haute cuisine kitchens until Peruvian chefs returned from working in Europe started to use them in Lima.

Razor clams receive minimal preparation in our kitchen as we serve them raw and fresh. We simply soak them in a purple corn reduction for 15 seconds in a vacuum sealed bag, which alters their colour while adding a touch of sweetness to balance out their inherent notes of iodine. We change their flavour without actually cooking them.

Razor clams are harvested twice a year in February and August.

STONE CRAB

Local fishermen say this non-endemic crustacean (Menippe mercenaria) came to Peru via massive fishing boats trawling from the Gulf of Mexico and the northern Atlantic Ocean. Found along Peru's coastline, the stone crab is totally at home in Paracas Bay, which is also home to bivalve molluscs. Crawling along the sea bed at a leisurely pace, it feasts on clams and razor clams: it's Paracas' greatest nemesis.

Its claws are especially strong: first, the stone crab identifies its potential meal and waits patiently for the scallop or razor clam to open its shell to breathe or eat. It then blocks the shell with one claw, holding it open while scooping out the flesh with the other.

A stone crab can eat up to 30 scallops a day – it's a true enemy of both bivalves and Paracas' artisanal fishermen, who, in addition to diving to collect bivalves, now work to control this crab's ever-growing population.

Young adult crabs especially thrive in Paracas Bay. Fishermen bag up any size in order to rid the bay of them.

Its sweet meat reflects its scallop diet, both tasty and subtle, it is in fact similar to eating a scallop.

Given that they are now a plague, the stone crab has now become part of the fishermen's daily diet.

In PARACAS, the second course of our Yachay tasting menu, we plate both the prey and their predator of the bay's whole ecosystem. We shred the crab meat and mix it with a razor clam emulsion. We also make a crab-based parihuela sauce, a typical Peruvian seafood-based stock, which is also mixed into the crab meat.

ALGAE: SEA LETTUCE AND YUYO

Sea lettuce (Ulva lactuca) and yuyo (Chondracanthus chamissoi) grow along many of the world's coastlines. We source these edible algae from Paracas, and sometimes use sargassum a brown macroalgae, as well as codium (Codium tomentosum), a macroalgae. Fishermen gather the bright green Ulva lactuca and Chondracanthus chamissoi, a red carragenophyte, from Paracas Bay's calm waters.

Yuyo is bursting with umami and has a firm, surprising texture that's almost like raw meat.

Sea lettuce's threads are thin and plastic in texture. It's easy to break apart. Yuyo can be easily stewed and when served fresh, is a natural companion in ceviche.

Sea lettuce has never been traditionally used in Peruvian cuisine and is a new addition.

We mix yuyo and sea lettuce together, blanching, grinding and dehydrating them, then make a crunchy cracker, making use of all of their gelling properties.

Sea lettuce and yuyo are harvested year round.

3 Aubergine

MOMENT THREE: BERENJENA

A member of the nightshade Solanaceae family, aubergine or eggplant is cultivated historically in Asia.
Aubergine is one of our firm favourites in the restaurant. It's one of the first vegetables we started to cultivate and understand in Yachay. I was in the seed store, deciding what to buy – carrots, pumpkins and potatoes among others – and it was the aubergine that best adapted to the land. Our culinary knowledge led us to harvest baby aubergines, when they barely have any seeds, so the pulp is fleshy.
Our agronomist Carlos Chipana cultivates what botanically is actually a berry.

Baby aubergine is meatier in texture than a full-size one and doesn't have seeds; its flavour is delicate.
Medium-size aubergine don't have that many seeds, which give off a bitter flavour, so we put them into our consommé.
We use large aubergines to make butter, and use its skin to create a cracker.
To make consommé, we lightly peel medium-sized aubergines and let them cry into salty water for 30 minutes, before rinsing them and making tiny holes in the flesh. They then sweat it out in a vacuum sealer at 75°C for three hours. Then we open the bags and let them decant, letting the broth run free.

4 Loche & Yellow chilli pepper

MOMENT FOUR: ZAPALLO

LOCHE

Sporting a bluish-green skin with the odd bump or two, loche can vary in shape, looking like butternut squash and taking on bottle shape or even crookneck forms.

Loche is one of Peru's 10 ingredients holding denomination of origin, which it was granted in 2010.

Given its high nutritional properties of beta-carotene and vitamins A and C, loche is considered to be a superfood.

We source loche from Lambayeque in Peru's northern coastal region.

It's a sweet squash, like sweet potato, with a creamy texture that hints at aniseed.

Here's a trick: to know that it's fresh, the stalk should not be dry.

A staple in northern Peruvian dishes, loche is used in seco de cabrito, a traditional goat stew, and in tortilla. It's very versatile.

We cook with two sizes: one kilo and 600 grams.

As the skin is more tender on the smaller 600-gram loche, we use that to make oil, serving it in small jugs at the table. We also peel the fresh seeds and serve them as part of the same course.

The large, one-kilo loche is used for a batido or a silky purée, and also in a salsa with yellow chilli peppers and huacatay leaves

YELLOW CHILLI PEPPER

One of Peru's essential ingredients, the ají amarillo or yellow chilli pepper has been cultivated for more than 6,500 years.

The first traces of this Capsicum baccatum were noted in the department of Ancash, located in the central northern Peru.

Today, ají amarillo is cultivated all over the country, between Ancash in the north and Tacna in the south.

Chillis in general have high nutritional values, and the ají amarillo is notable for vitamins A, B6 and C, as well as its iron, magnesium and potassium content. They also metabolise fats and help to reduce low-density lipoprotein or bad cholesterol by acting as a natural fat burner.

This chilli packs a punch: its spiciness ranges between 30,000 and 50,000 Scoville Heat Units.

We buy from producers in Ancash and Moquegua, choosing chillies with an elongated shape that are spicy and aromatic.

While ají amarillo is commonly used to make sauces and sautéed dishes, we also use it as a base for emulsions so as to add aroma and spicy flavours. It's most flavourful, and its intense orangey-yellow hue boosts any dish's colour.

5 Giant white corn, red quinoa & Panca chilli pepper

MOMENT FIVE: CHOCLOS

GIANT WHITE CORN (DO)

This heirloom giant white corn is only cultivated in the Sacred Valley between 2,600 and 3,050 metres above sea level. It grows in five of the seven districts in the province of Urubamba, and six of the seven in the province of Calca.

Endemic to Peru, giant white corn has had Denominación de Origen or a certificate of origin since 2005, and is one of 10 such Peruvian ingredients.

Its size makes it notable. The plant can grow up to three metres tall (the average is two) and produces a cob that's twice as large as a regular one, with kernels three times bigger. This means the plant packs more nutrients than other varieties: high in vitamin D, it's considered to be a super food.

When you eat giant white corn raw, it's sweet and juicy because of the large kernels, and also a little milky, with a light earthy flavour. Bite into it: the kernels explode in your mouth.

We work with a co-operative based in Urubamba, which cultivates the corn, and we receive it fresh at the end of the rainy season in April. When it's out of season, we buy dehydrated corn then use it in different ways for the rest of the year.

The soleada technique naturally dehydrates cobs and the kernels are used to make cancha, toasted corn usually used in cebiche.

We use giant white corn in every possible way, for example, the dried used cobs are easily combustible so we use them as tinder.

As for the pancas or husks, we oven roast them until they are black then turn them into an ash, which, although savoury, is also curiously sweet.

After extracting starch and corn milk from fresh cobs, we create a foam.

We even use the hairy parts of the cob, dehydrating them to make crunchy tendrils.

RED QUINUA

An Andean cereal par excellence, quinua has been cultivated for thousands of years.

A hardy crop in the amaranth family that withstands the extremely frigid cold of the Andes at 4,000 metres above sea level, it has long sustained Andean communities who developed techniques to store it.

A distinctive towering and flowering crop, its tiny seeds hold powerful nutritional values such as protein, fibre and vitamin B, providing vital nutrients to Andean inhabitants who aren't able to cultivate fresh vegetables or fruit at such elevation.

Seeds are sown in September and October and require lots of water; harvest takes place in April.

Quinua is so high in protein – double that of other crops – that the NASA space agency uses it in cereal bars.

In traditional Andean cooking, quinua is used in soups and broths, with a little sugar or cinnamon. One popular soup is quinua with chuño, perhaps supplemented with alpaca jerky, or a guiso stew with cheese and chilli peppers.

Quinua hasn't always been popular: in recent times it was replaced by European cereals leading to dwindling regular consumption in Peru. Fortunately this superfood started to make a comeback at the start of the 21st century.

Producing a rainbow array of seeds from orange, yellow, red and violet, we make the most of these vibrant colours to lift dishes.

By dehydrating red quinua flowers, we can pigment sauces.

We use this versatile crop in a number of ways, such as enhancing the escabeche's colour.

PANCA CHILLI PEPPER

Peruvians traditionally cook with three popular ajies or chilli peppers: Limo, which is used fresh in cebiche and is cultivated along the Pacific coast; the Andean Rocoto, which is dried; and the Panca, a red chilli pepper that is also from the coast, specifically from Chiclayo in the northwest province of Lambayeque.

Panca chilli pepper forms part of the core of all sofritos (sautéed aromatics). All sofritos start with garlic and onion. A yellow one draws from ají amarillo, a green one from coriander leaves, while a red one uses ají panca. It's also a core ingredient of the anticucho sauce.

Intense dark red in colour, panca has medium spice levels, its pungency measuring between 1,000 and 1,500 Scoville Heat Units.

Usually dried in the sun, this Capsicum chinense takes on burgundy and chocolate brown hues once dehydrated. Cinnamon-like in aroma, panca has sweet and acidic notes.

Harvest time comes twice a year, between February and April then between July and September.

Ají panca naturally forms the base to Mayta's sofritos, but we toast it over hot coals to open it up then remove the seeds. We then triple cook it in boiling water, changing the liquid each time to remove any excess heat. It then forms part of the base of the quinua escabeche.

6 Carachama, Tacupí & Charapita chilli pepper

MOMENT SIX: PECES AMAZÓNICOS

CARACHAMA

This Amazonian armoured catfish is widely consumed in the Amazon regions of Loreto, San Martín, Guanaco, Ucayal and Madre de Dios.

Due to its hard, rigid scales and sunken eyes, its appearance is rather prehistoric.

This species easily adapts to new habitats, particularly to shallow rocky waters.

In the jungle, carachama is traditionally boiled for a long time, so as to penetrate the scales and reach the meat, then served in soup.

Its meat is considered to be a superfood given that it's 19 percent protein and also rich in vitamins A, C, E and B12, as well as phosphorus, iron and iodine.

We work with artisanal fishermen from Iquitos who catch carachama for the restaurant.

November is spawning season and in the kitchen we cure carachama roe just like sturgeon caviar, then stuff a cassava fritter with it. Notable for its orange-yellow colour, it's very tasty.

We also use the entire fish, slow baking it in the oven for 18 hours to create rather unique aquatic dishware.

The tail also serves its purpose: we cure it for seven days then smoke it to make a fishtail ham.

GAMITANA

The largest fish in the Characidae family, the gamitana lives in the Amazon basin and is known as tambaquí in Spanish and black pacu.

While its piranha cousin feasts on flesh, gamitana mostly feeds on fruits, seeds and some zooplankton.

Thanks to this herbivore-led diet, gamitana expels fruit seeds in rivers, playing its part in regenerating submerged Amazon forests.

This lobe-finned fish is a popular species thanks to its delicious flavour, but it's been overfished, so we only purchase it from an Amazon fish farm, thereby supporting such enterprises in the region.

Its lobe fins are hard to clean because they have an enormous number of encrusted barbs, but as it's so versatile, it's worth the effort.

After removing the spiky lobes and skin, we air dry the skin separately then put it back together with fish protein and seal it. The skin takes on a very crispy texture that contrasts with the tender juicy loin.

TUCUPÍ

An extract taken from the wild manioc root or yuca brava, tucupí is fermented to make an intense yellow-coloured sauce.

Yuca brava requires careful processing because it is naturally high in cyanide. Communities in Bora and Huitoto in the Pucaurquillo area in the basin of the Apayacu and Ampiacu rivers, about four hours from Iquitos in the Amazon basin, cultivate yuca brava. The people from these two communities taught us how to prepare it.

After it's harvested, you clean the yuca brava then peel, grate and squeeze it to separate the liquid. Once grated, you can then use the liquid and pulp. The pulp is used to make flour, by drying it. The juice is left to rest so that the yuca brava starch settles and once it has slightly fermented, it becomes cassava or tapioca. The remaining liquid is cooked very gently for around seven days over a very low heat. The yuca brava's remaining starch, sugar and toxic cyanide content are removed and the liquid becomes even more concentrated.

Depending on the number of days it is cooked and fermented, tucupí acquires different characteristics and levels of concentration. When it take on a liquid soft oily texture, its flavou are citrus and herbaceous with some umami taste. When it becomes more concentrated, spice and coffee notes appear along with a slightly nutty bitterness.

When it takes on bitter notes, the Bo and Huitoto communities call it ají negro and use it to season stews and fish. In our kitchen, we flavour tucup with charapita chilli pepper, sacha cu lantro (coriander cultivated in the Am azon) and tree tomato to balance its bitterness and create our version of a thick and intense barbecue sauce.

CHARAPITA CHILLI PEPPER

The most appreciated Capsicum tha grows in the Peruvian Amazon, the small round yellow charapita chilli pepper boasts wonderful flavours an aromas backed up by great bite that isn't too spicy.

Cultivated in both the high jungle ar of San Martín and the low-lying jungle area of Iquitos, charapita grown i San Martín has more intense aroma while the latter stands out for its intense bite.

The fruit is harvested during the rainy season between December an March, which is when charapita chillies are in their maximum splendou In Amazon communities, it is used t make fresh sauces or simply choppe up to accompany a main dish.

In the kitchen, we smoke it then add it to citrus emulsions and infusions t give them spicy and smoky notes. W also dehydrate charapita chillies to make spicy and aromatic powders.

7 Alpaca, Andean herbs & Olluco

MOMENT SEVEN: ALPACA

ALPACA

A direct descendent of the vicuña, the alpaca is a South American camelid that was first domesticated around 6,000 years ago.
A lean and high-protein meat that's low in fat, alpaca is also high in omega-3 and omega-6.
We work with small ranchers in Puno and Juliaca in southern Peru, who raise animals to two- to a maximum of three-years old, weighing no more than 75 kilos to ensure tender meat.
Traditionally, alpaca was dried in the sun for up to 20 days to make charqui or jerky, although it also benefits from slow cooking at low temperatures.
In the kitchen, we slowly stew the legs at a low temperature to tenderise them, boosting the flavour with aromatics such as carrots, onions, leeks and turnips. Once stewed, we further break down the meat in its own cooking juices, so that even the collagen becomes extremely soft.

ANDEAN HERBS

2.1 Chincho

This aromatic herb is cultivated in the Andes, and has sweet notes to it.
While chincho's leaves are similar in shape to those of huacatay, its subtle aromas embrace hints of lemon, mint, basil and tarragon.
A versatile herb, chincho easily adapts to meat stews, sauces and the typical uchucuta salsas found in traditional Andean cuisine.
Chincho willingly shares its aromas, so we perfume demi-glace sauces – such as reduced alpaca juices – with its stalks.
We process its leaves to make an intense green broth, which also includes huacatay, muña, paico and common rue. This is a dish that's typically made in the Central Sierras region.

2.2 Huacatay

An aromatic herb cultivated in the Andes, huacatay's aromas fall between basil and mint with a hint of tarragon.
A member of the Asteraceae family, it's also known as chinchilla and, in Spanish, suico, or Southern Cone Marigold.
Cultivated for Mayta in Tarma, in Peru's Central Sierras region, it's traditionally added to lift a dish's aroma, such as ocopa sauce that originates from Arequipa, and Andean stews.
Huacatay's mint-like leaves are medicinally powerful, producing an anti-fungal essential oil.
We also cultivate huacatay in Yachay, our organic garden, where it acts as a natural pest repellent. We process its leaves to create an intensely green liquid that we then mix with other herbs to create a green broth.

2.3 Paico

Paico stands out for its long leaves and intense aroma that bears earthy notes. This perennial herb is also known as payqu, epazote, mastruz and herbs sanctæ Mariæ in Spanish, and Jesuit's tea or Mexican tea. Paico's medicinal properties help to relieve indigestion and stomach aches.
In Peruvian cooking, it's traditionally used in stews and tamales but, above all, in meat stews. One typical dish is paico green soup made the Cajamarca way.

2.4 Common rue

A medicinal plant, in small doses ruda or common rue can help to cure sore throats, headaches and bring down high temperatures.
It is also a popular herb used in shamanic ceremonies and rituals, and is a symbol of good fortune in Peru.
Common rue has a curiously oily aroma that combines with earthy notes.

2.5 Muña

Known as Andean mint, muña is a vital medicinal plant used in teas and infusions.
It is often consumed to prevent or he[illegible] cure stomach ache.
Muña is aromatically intense with strong menthol fragrances.
In traditional cooking, muña is used Andean soups or lamb a la muña.
In the kitchen we process its leaves with huacatay, chincho, paico and common rue to make our green broth.

OLLUCO

A native Andean tuber whose pigmentations can be pink, red and yellow, olluco or ullucus was domesticated by ancient settlers in the high plateau u[illegible] to 4,000 metres above sea level.
In Peru, olluco is mostly cultivated in the Cusco region although it also grows in the Ayacucho area.
It's usually harvested between June and August, but today at different altitudes, and in different microclimates it can be cultivated year round.
On 5 October, several Andean communities celebrate this tuber with the D[illegible] del olluquito, or Little Olluco Day.
Olluco is a hardy tuber that can be stored for several months after it's pulled from the ground.
In ancestral cooking, it is boiled and served with alpaca jerky.
Nutritional values include vitamin A and betalain, an antioxidant found in some pigmentations. Its fibre and viscous mucilage levels can also help to control cholesterol.
In the kitchen we cook olluco at a low temperature vegetable fat or butter to make a silky smoothie, then boost it with some characteristic Andean herb[illegible]
We also cut it into spheres, then whitewash it with a meat or mushroom broth so it keeps its crunchines[illegible]

8 Macambo, Copoazú, Arazá & Amazonian Melipona honey

MOMENT EIGHT: AMAZÓNICO

MACAMBO

A member of the Theobroma family that includes cacao, macambo's scientific name is Theobroma bicolor.
Its wrinkly pod is filled with highly nutritive beans packed with fibre, protein and omega-9.
Native to the Amazon region, we source macambo from the cloud forests of San Martín in Tarapoto.
In the kitchen, we toast the beans then candy them.
Once toasted, we also make emulsions and milks for the Amazónico dessert.

COPOAZÚ

Theobroma grandiflorum, more commonly known as copoazú, is a member of the cacao family and is one of the tallest-growing trees in the Theobroma genus.
Its mucilage is denser than that of its cacao cousin, and has intense aromas with lactic yoghurt notes. This gelatinous solution contributes to copoazú's citrus flavour.
Our copoazú is cultivated in the Selva Alta de Tarapoto, Moyobamba, in the Amazon region.
Highly versatile, we use copoazú pulp to make sorbets and clouds, while we process the seeds to make butter.

ARAZÁ

This yellow-hued smooth-skinned fruit comes from a small shrub and is similar to guava.
The size of an apple, arazá has light lactic aromas while its flavour is citrus.
Its pale-yellow pulp is thick and juicy.
Arazá grows in the rainforest; we source it from the Ucayali region.
While its pulp is traditionally used to make refreshing beverages, in the kitchen we make an arazá cloud that's like a meringue.

AMAZONIAN MELIPONA HONEY

Melipona honey is produced by wild stingless bees that are much smaller in size than other bees.
A powerful natural restorative, this gooey delight has particularly citrus flavours and very floral aromas such as orange blossom.
We work closely with a beekeeper in Moyobamba – known as the city of orchids – in San Martín in the Amazon region, who manages around 12 stingless bee species.
Melipona honey is prized for its high quality; its texture is more liquid than traditional honey while its flavours are more intense.

9 Tumbo

MOMENT NINE: TUMBO

Tumbo, known as banana passion-fruit in English, is one of Peru's ancient fruits that has been consumed since the pre-Columbian era.
A member of the passion fruit family, the Inca civilisation appreciated this rather surprising fruit that looks like a rather straight yellowy-green banana, but when sliced open is full of juicy pulp and seeds, just like a common passion fruit.
Abundant in vitamin C, tumbo is a lot sweeter than its passion fruit sibling, not as slimy in texture and has more compact seeds.
It's most at home growing in high-elevation cloud forests between 1,400 and 2,000 metres above sea level.
We source our tumbo from small farms located close to Lima in Huarochirí province. As the plants are creeping vines, farmers treat them like tomatoes, coercing them to grow up along trellises.
In the kitchen, we make the most of tumbo's pectin extracted from the peel's pith.
While it's delicious made in smoothies or eaten raw, we like to use it to make tumbo sorbet. As for the peel itself, which is rich in fibre, we dehydrate it to create hot infusions.

10 Tunta & Yacon

MOMENT TEN: TUNTA

TUNTA

Tunta also goes by the name of chuño blanco, but both names for this freeze-dried white potato refer to an ancestral preservation technique that is still commonly used in the high plateau today. Andean communities living at 3,200 metres above sea level and higher apply a low temperature dehydration or lyophilisation process to Andean potatoes.

Lyophilised potatoes can easily be stored, allowing people living in these remote elevated communities to have continual food sources year round.

There are several steps involved in preparing tunta. First, farmers leave potatoes to freeze on a bed of straw, making the most of the extreme change in thermal range. June day temperatures might reach 18°C, when high solar radiation helps to dry out tubers, but by night they can fall to -12°C – and that's when the potatoes freeze.

During this process, which lasts between five and seven days, the potatoes lose their liquids. They are then transferred in mesh nets to river shallows, where the current rushes over them, slowly changing the texture and colour.

Once removed from the river, the tunta is dried and peeled, then left for five more days to the Pachamama's whims, until they are totally white.

Tunta is traditionally used in dishes such as stews and vegetable soup.

In Mayta's kitchen, we use it in its natural state, grating it to make the most of its lightly lactic, and at times salty, flavour.

Another use for tunta is bringing together fresh tubers such as papa ambo –a small native potato– with a chilli pepper emulsion, then covering it with just-grated tunta to give it a creamy touch.

YACON

A perennial orange-coloured daisy that belongs to the Asteraceae family, yacón is in fact appreciated for its tasty roots and is considered to be a tuber.

A warm weather lover, yacón is cultivated at between 1,200 and 1,400 metres above sea level on the edge of the jungle.

A crunchy root, bite into a raw yacón and its texture immediately reminds you of an apple. But, in difference to those fruits from the Malus genus, it's simply sweet without much acidity.

In contrast to other tubers, yacón doesn't bear much starch and lacks the earthy notes we are accustomed to.

Our yacón is sourced from the eastern jungle region.

In Mayta's kitchen, we cut the yacón into small cubes that are barely cooked before they are served, then extract liquid from the rest. We reduce that liquid to obtain a honey, with which we lacquer a lightly cooked yacón. As it stays crunchy, with subtle lightly sweet flavours, it creates an ideal interval between the savoury and sweet stages of the tasting menu.

11 Pacae

MOMENT ELEVEN: MUCÍLAGO

Going by an array of names such as the ice-cream bean tree, guaba and pepeto, pacae is native to South America. Growing tall on the edge of the jungle, its fruit is a long curved pod, like an oversize bean. When you open it up, it has a row of black seeds covered in white mucilage that looks like cotton wool.

When it's in season, we source it from the Huarochirí region but it can also come from Ayacucho as well as Urubamba Valley.

Pacae is sweet and aromatic. The seed is rather astringent but its soft, cloud-like mucilage is sweet and has good acidity.

As it's so special, we tend to let the pacae speak for itself.

We clean the fruit then fill it with cacao mucilage, thereby creating a course that focuses on different mucilages.

SECTION_6_MAY

A EXPERIENCE

The Mayta experience is made up of 11 moments that highlight the multiplicity of ingredients that reflect the complex and vast identity of Peru.

1 Tubérculos

MOMENT ONE

1 servi

INGREDIENTS

Slices from 1 confit ambo potato
15 g White onion, sautéed
8 g Egg yolk emulsion
5 g Tunta
Pinch Salt

PREPARATION

1 Fry the potato for 2 minutes until golden then remove excess oil. Stack the slices, then, from the top, cut a small well in the middle of the slices. **2** Combine the sautéed onion and yolk emulsion, and adjust the salt. **3** Fill the well in the potato with the onion mixture. **4** Grate the tunta over the top using a Microplane or fine grater.

————

Part 1: Confit Potatoes (yield: 17)

250 g Ambo cocktail potatoes
10 g Salt
25 g Butter
10 g Rosemary
25 ml Olive oil

1 Use a mandoline to cut the potatoes into 1 mm slices. **2** Arrange the slices on a sheet of aluminium foil, season with salt, pepper and rosemary, and add the olive oil and butter. **3**. Bake in the oven for 10 minutes at 180°C. **4** After removing the potato slices, freeze them for 12 hours before frying them.

Part 2: Sautéed White Onion

500 g White onion, cleaned
150 g Olive oil
15 g Salt
5 tsp. Black pepper

1 Finely feather-cut the onions and transfer to a saucepan with the olive oil. **2** Stir while cooking until the onion is translucent. Season with salt and pepper. **3** Once done, use a strainer to remove the excess liquid and set the onions aside.

Part 3: Egg Yolk Emulsion (yield: 340 g)

95 g Egg yolks
4 g Salt
200 g Olive oil
2 g Black pepper
10 g Onion oil

1 Place the egg yolks in a Thermomix, set the temperature to 65°C and the speed to 6. **2** Add the oil in a thin, steady drizzle. **3** Adjust the seasoning. **4** Process for about 7 minutes until the emulsion is uniform and has a good density. Set aside.

2 Paracas

1 servi

MOMENT TWO

INGREDIENTS

1 Scallop, cleaned
2 g Scallop coral escabeche sauce
3 g Scallop bottarga, grated
1 ml Algae oil
1 ml Annatto oil
10 g Fava bean mousse
4 Calendula flower heads
4 Sprigs coriander
4 Purple pansy flower heads
20 ml Scallop leche de tigre
80 g Sea lettuces, mixed varieties

PREPARATION

1 Dress the scallop in its shell with the coral escabeche sauce and add the grated bottarga. Garnish with the calendula, coriander and pansies **2** Add the fava bean mousse to the base of the shell, then add the scallop milk **3** Add 3 dots each of the algae and annatto oils. **4** Prepare a plate with crushed ice, add the sea lettuces, and arrange the garnished scallop on top.

————

Leche de Tigre (yield 2.5 L)

300 g Ginger
440 g Celery
100 g Ají limo (lemon drop chilli pepper)
100 g Red onion
100 g Garlic cloves
30 g Coriander stems
1.5 L Lime juice
600 ml Fish meat scraps
600 ml Fish stock
20 g Salt
100 g Ají charapita (wild Peruvian chilli pepper)

1 With the exception of the xanthan gum and oil, combine and process all the ingredients in a blender, then strain through a kitchen sieve or cheesecloth. **2** Gradually mix in the xanthan gum and oil to the liquid to give it body and texture. Adjust the seasoning, cover and refrigerate until ready for use.

Scallop Coral Escabeche (yield 150 g)

150 ml Escabeche base
64 g Scallop coral (roe)
10 ml Vegetable oil
25 g Butter
30 ml Pisco
2 ml White vinegar
2 g Salt

1 Sauté the coral in butter, deglaze the pan with pisco and season with salt. **2** Transfer the sautéed coral to a blender and add the escabeche base, vinegar and oil and process. **3** Strain the mixture and refrigerate until ready for use.

Scallop Bottarga (yield 1.6 kg)

20 g Abanico scallop coral
4 kg Sugar
4 kg Salt

1 Combine the sugar and salt and mix well. **2** Transfer half the sugar and salt mixture to a large serving platter or baking pan, then the coral, then cover with the other half of the mixture, and let sit for 45 minutes. **3** Rinse off the coral and drain away any excess liquid. **4** Spread the coral on a Silpat and dry overnight at 55°C.

Annatto Oil (yield 600 ml)

100 g Annatto seeds
600 ml Vegetable oil

Heat the oil and annatto over medium heat until the oil is infused with colour; be careful not to to simmer or approach a boil. Allow to cool for 10 minutes then strain and set aside.

Algae Oil (yield 100 ml)

7 g Blanched algae
100 ml Vegetable oil
4 g Kale
5 g Cilantro

1 Liquify the ingredients in a blender and filter through a cheesecloth. **2** Allow the mixture to steep for a day to develop colour. **3** Cover and refrigerate until ready for use.

Coral Crisp 1 Serving

1 Coral crisp
7 g Fava mousse
1 Calendula flower
1 Coriander sprout
1 Purple aster
2 g Scallop emulsion
2 Coriander flowers

Pipe some mousse atop the crip, the garnish with some dots of the scallop emulsion, flower petals, the spro and some fava beans.

Scallop Emulsion (yield: 450 g)

102 g Egg
360 g Vegetable oil
100 g Leche de tigre
72 g Sautéed scallops
30 g Limo (lemon drop) chilli
5 g Salt
50 g Smoke oil
9 g Xanthan gum
1 g Lemon juice

1 Make mayonnaise base in a blender with the egg and vegetable oil. **2** Then add the scallops and the other ingredients except the smoke oil and xanthan gum. Mix until uniform. **3** Finish by giving it texture and body with the smoke oil and xanthan gum. Adjust the seasoning.

Coral Crisp (yield: 500 g)
50 g Scallop coral
300 g Cassava, cooked
250 g Rice, cooked
1 g Salt
150 g Aderezo de rojo (a sofrito)
100 g Fava bean crisp

1 With the exception of the fava crisp, transfer all the ingredients to a Thermomix, set the speed at 6 and process for about 5 minutes. **2** Once the mixture is uniform and smooth, spread it on a silicone mat and lay pieces of the bean crisp on top to give it a dual tone. Wait for it to dry, then fry 15 g pieces in 180°C vegetable oil.

Aderezo (Sofrito Base) (yield: 1 kg)
800 g white onion
200 g garlic
100 g vegetable oil

Heat the oil and fry the brunoise chopped garlic. Once it's very soft, add the chopped onion and leave to caramelise on a low heat, crush and reserve.

Fava Bean Mousse (yield: 1 kg)
0.9 kg Fava beans, cooked
50 g Aderezo base (sofrito)
30 g Butter
40 g Coriander oil
40 g Milk
8 g Salt

1 Add all the ingredients to a saucepan to heat through and mix. **2** Transfer to a Thermomix and process until smooth and uniform.

Aderezo (Sofrito Base) (yield: 1.5 kg)
800 g white onion
200 g garlic
800 g panca chilli pepper paste
100 g vegetable oil

Heat the oil and fry the brunoise chopped garlic. Once it's very soft, add the chopped onion and leave to caramelise on a low heat, add the panca chilli pepper paste, and leave that to caramelise further. Process it and keep back.

Aji Panca Paste (yield: 800 g)
4 kg dried panca chilli peppers
Water as required

Slice the chillies lengthways and remove the seeds with a knife.
Fill a pan with cold water and bring the chillies to a fast boil then quickly strain them, filling the pan with fresh cold water. Repeat this step four times until they are no longer spicy.
Strain the chillies and crush them to a paste, and hold back.

Fava Bean Crisp (yield: 200 g)
100 g Fava beans, cooked
200 g Cassava, cooked
40 g Kale, blanched and shocked
150 g Rice, cooked
1 g salt

1 Transfer the kale to a Thermomix and process until it becomes a paste. **2** Add the other ingredients, set the speed to 6 and process for about 5 minutes. **3** Once the mixture is uniform and smooth, spread it on a silicone mat and dehydrate until it becomes papery. Fry 15 g pieces in 180°C vegetable oil.

Algae Crisp & Crab (1 serving)
1 Algae cylinder crisp
15 g Crab meat, cooked
5 g Osmotic razor clams
2 g Yuyo (red algae) crisp
5 g Razor clam emulsion

1 Sauté the razor clams in olive oil and a little salt. **2** Fill the algae cylinder with the crab meat. **3** Cover both ends with the emulsion. **4** Slice the osmotic razor clams and place 3 slices on the crisp. **5** Finish with a decorative yuyo crisp.

Algae Crisps (yield: 100 cylinders)
1 kg Sea lettuce, blanched and shocked
600 g Cassava, cooked
300 g Rice, cooked

1 Process all the ingredients together in a Thermomix set at 6 speed and 70°C. Spread the mixture on a silicone mat and score 6 cm x 6 cm squares. **2** Form a cylinder with each square and fry in 180°C vegetable oil.

Razor Clam Emulsion (yield: 500 g)
102 g Egg
360 g Vegetable oil
100 g Leche de tigre
72 g Razor clams, sautéed
30 g Limo (lemon drop) chillies
20 g Salsa parihuela
5 g Salt
50 g Smoke oil
10 g Xanthan gum

1 Make mayonnaise base in a blender with the egg and vegetable oil. **2** Then add the razor clams and the other ingredients except the smoke oil and xanthan gum. Mix until uniform. **3** Finish by giving it texture and body with the smoke oil and xanthan gum. Adjust the seasoning.

Clam Tart (1 serving)
1 Green tartlet shell
8 g Clam filling
15 g Broccoli cream
20 g Broccoli couscous
5 g Baby asparagus, bias-cut

1 Pipe the broccoli cream into the tartlet shell, followed by the clam filling and decorate the top with brocco-

ouscous. **2** To finish, arrange the paragus in a circular shape.

roccoli Cream (yield: 400 g)
30 g Broccoli
0 g Aderezo base (sofrito)
g Salt
0 g Olive oil
0 g Confit garlic

Blanch the broccoli in a saucepan en transfer to a blender along with e oil, salt, aderezo base and con- garlic. Process until the mixture is niform and smooth. **2** Transfer to a stry bag and reserve.

roccoli Couscous (yield: 250 g)
00 g Broccoli

Use a knife to carefully cut the buds f the florets, then transfer it to a tray ned with a damp WypAll cloth and t aside. **2** Use a kitchen torch to ntly cook the broccoli, being mindful ot to burn it.

am Tartare (yield: 350 g)
30 g Clams
g Salt
g Lemon juice
0 g Razor clam emulsion

ut the clams into 5 mm cubes, trans- to a bowl and mix in the other ingre- ents. Store in an airtight container.

Tartlet Shells (yield: 32 shells)
60 g Powdered mushrooms
80 g Powdered algae
350 g Butter
15 g Phyllo dough (5 sheets)

1 Melt the butter with the powders then transfer to a blender and pro- cess until the powders have dissolved and the colour is uniform. **2** Cut the phyllo sheets into 4 equal parts, brush each sheet with butter and layer, be- ing very careful not to tear the dough. Be sure not to allow air between the layers. **3** Use a circular cutter to cut rounds and place them in tart- let moulds. Trim off the corners and freeze for 20 minutes. **4** Bake for 8 minutes until they are crispy. Allow to cool and set aside.

3 Berenjena

MOMENT THREE

1 servi

INGREDIENTS

100 ml Aubergine consommé
1 Grilled baby aubergine
10 Drops fennel oil
1 tsp. Crispy shallot
2 g Citrus aioli
30 g Aubergine cream
2 g Purple aster petals
1 tsp. Smoked maltodextrin
5 ml Black garlic sauce
10 g Aubergine crisps

PREPARATION

1 Start by searing a baby aubergine on a hot griddle. Transfer to a shallow bowl and make a straight line down its length with the black garlic sauce and the aioli. Garnish with crispy shallot and purple aster petals. **2** Arrange a quenelle of aubergine cream on a stone along with sprinkling of crispy aubergine and garnish with a dusting of smoked maltodextrin powder. **3** Heat and adjust the seasoning of the aubergine consommé and transfer to a warmed ceramic sauce server. Pour into the bowl at the time of serving.

———

Aubergine Consommé (yield: 500 g)

500 ml Aubergine broth
40 g Sugar
10 pinches Coarse salt

1 After making the aubergine broth, strain and set it aside. **2** Caramelise the sugar in a saucepan, add the broth and stir constantly. **3** Season with salt and set aside.

Aubergine Broth (yield: 4 kg)

20 kg Aubergines

Peel the aubergines (reserve the skins for later recipe) and transfer the aubergines to 2 kg sous vide bags and seal. Cook for 1 hour at 90°C (195°F), then slit the bags to pour out the resulting broth into a container. Avoid squeezing or pressing the bag as that will darken the liquid.

Grilled Baby Aubergine (yield: 24)

24 Baby aubergines
2 L Water
100 g Coarse salt
14 g Ascorbic acid
400 g Wood chips
2 kg Charcoal
30 g Rosemary

1 For the brine, stir in 50 grams salt in 1 litre of water. **2** Wash and peel the aubergines then immerse them in the brine for about 40 minutes. **3** For the ascorbic acid solution, combine 7 grams of ascorbic acid per 1 litre of water and reserve. **4** Fill 4 sous vide bags with 6 baby aubergines each, add 250 ml of the ascorbic acid solution to each bag and seal. **5** Steam the bags at 85°C for 1 hour. **6** Remove the aubergines from the bags and smoke using the wood shavings, charcoal and rosemary for about 20 minutes and set aside.

Fennel Oil (yield 150 g)

150 ml Vegetable oil
250 g Fennel fronds

1 Remove the fronds from the fennel bulb, then wash and blanch them. **2** Blend the ingredients, filte through a cheesecloth and set aside.

Crispy Shallot (yield 1.2 kg)

1.8 kg Shallots, sliced crosswise
500 g Bread flour
20 g Icing sugar
30 g Coarse salt
10 g Garlic powder
Vegetable oil for frying

1 Mix together the dry ingredients. **2** Dredge the sliced shallots in the mixture and gently shake off any excess. **3** Fry the shallots 180°C oil until golden and crisp, drain the excess oil and set the shallots aside.

Citrus Aioli (yield 350 g)

4 Free-range egg yolks
30 g Citrus zest
1 tsp. Coarse salt
280 ml Vegetable oil
5 g Garlic confit
50 ml Extra virgin olive oil
1 dash Lemon juice

1 Prepare a mayonnaise base by combining the yolks and garlic confit and while blending, adding the vegetable oil in a steady stream. **2** Season with salt and lemon juice. **3** Finish by emulsifying in the olive oil and the fold in the citrus zest.

Aubergine Cream (yield 3.9 kg)
4.6 kg Aubergine
100 ml Honey
160 g Mayonnaise
500 g Black garlic sauce
50 ml Soy sauce
70 ml sesame oil
20 g Salt
10 g Sugar
200 ml Oyster sauce
Softened butter and olive oil for roasting

1 Wash and coarsely chop the aubergine, combine with enough butter and olive oil to lightly coat, and roast in a 220°C oven for 30 minutes until golden brown and cooked through. **2** Transfer the aubergine to a Thermomix and process at 60%, then remove and set aside. **3** Afterwards, separately process the honey, mayonnaise, black garlic sauce, soy sauce, oyster sauce, sesame oil, salt and sugar. **4** Combine the processed ingredients in a bowl, adjust the seasoning and set aside.

Aubergine Crisps (yield 200 g)
500 g Aubergine trimmings (peels)
100 g Rice
250 ml Purple corn extract
500 ml Water

1 Add the ingredients to a pot and cook until somewhat thickened. **2** Process in a blender or food processor, then strain. **3** Spread the mixture evenly on a Silpat and dehydrate at 60°C. When the preparation is ready, deep-fry at 180°C then allow to drain before serving.

Smoked Maltodextrin (yield 40 g)
30 g Maltodextrin
10 ml Charcoal oil
1 Pinch salt

Combine the dry ingredients in a bowl and use a whisk to mix in the slowly added oil.

Black Garlic Sauce (yield 1 kg)
100 g Black garlic
3 Free-range egg yolks
300 ml Vegetable oil
30 ml Soy sauce
25 ml Sesame oil
80 ml Oyster sauce
100 ml Salsa macha (árbol chilli sauce)
100 ml Tucupi sauce
15 g Salt

1 Prepare a mayonnaise base with the egg yolks and vegetable oil and salsa macha. **2** Mix in the remaining ingredients until the sauce is uniform. **3** Adjust seasoning and reserve.

Charcoal Oil (yield 5 kg)
5 kg Vegetable oil, frozen
500 g Charcoal

1 Heat the charcoal until red hot, about 25 minutes. **2** Transfer the frozen oil to a large pot with a lid, very carefully add the heated charcoal, cover, wrap the top with cling film, then allow to cool.

4 Zapallos

MOMENT FOUR

1 servi

INGREDIENTS

25 g Macre squash spaghetti
2 g Huacatay and loche squash oil
50 g Loche squash curry
1 g Pumpkin seeds
1 g Sunflower seeds
1 g Huacatay buds
1 g Orange marigold
10 g Loche squash purée
Carrot gel, as needed
Pumpkin gel, as needed
Pickled pumpkin fibres, as needed

PREPARATION

1 Sauté the spaghetti in olive oil, salt and set aside. **2** Heat the curry sauce in a saucepan, mix in lemon juice, salt, huacatay and loche oil and set aside. **3** Add some huacatay and loche oil in a heated squash server, followed by the curry sauce. **5** Plate the loche purée, arrange the 'spaghetti' around it to form a corona, then decorate with lines of loche purée, the carrot and pumpkin gels, sunflower and pumpkin seeds, flowers and huacatay buds.

————

Loche Squash Curry (yield: 3 kg)

25 g Curry powder
2 kg Smoked cream
1.2 kg Loche purée
20 g Salt

1 Heat the smoked cream in a saucepan, mix in the loche purée. **2** Add a little cream to the curry powder, mix well and add it to the saucepan. Stir well and continuously to fully incorporate the powder. **3** Season with salt and set aside.

Huacatay & Loche Oil (yield: 800 g)

400 g Huacatay, leaves only
800 g Vegetable oil
100 g Loche squash skin

1 Peel the loche squash, preserving the peel. **2** Blanch and shock the huacatay, then wring and shake it dry. **3** Process the ingredients together in a Thermomix set at speed 8 for 8 minutes until all the fibre breaks down. **4** Pass it through cheesecloth or fine strainer, allow to cool. Set aside.

Loche Squash Purée (yield: 1 kg)

150 g Aderezo base
250 g Milk
1.2 kg Loche squash, baked
20 g Salt
22 g Sugar
120 g Light cream
30 g Unsalted butter
Olive oil, as needed

1 Peel and cut up the loche, transfer it to a baking sheet with butter and olive oil and cook at 180°C for 30 minutes. **2** When the loche is cooked, process it in a Thermomix with the other ingredients. **3** Adjust the seasoning and set aside.

Smoked Cream (yield: 1.5 kg)

2 kg Light cream
700 g Charcoal

1 Light the charcoal. **2** Pour the cream into a deep pot. When the charcoal is glowing red, transfer it into the pot, put the lid on immediately and weigh it down so the smoke doesn't escape. **3** Leave the pot unopened fo 4 hours, then set it aside.

Aderezo Base (sofrito) (yield: 0.8 kg

0.8 kg White onion
200 g Confit garlic
100 g Vegetable oil

1 Finely chop the white onion and sauté in oil. **2** When the onion is translucent, add the confit garlic and stir until golden brown, then set aside to cool.

Loche Squash 'Spaghetti' (yield: 1 kg)

1 kg Loche squash

1 Peel the pumpkin. **2** Use a vegetable peeler to make long slices of pumpkin, even out the ends so the slices are about the same size, then cut 2 mm-wide strands. Divide in 30-gram portions.

Pumpkin Gel (yield: 2 kg)
3.52 kg Orange pumpkin
20 g Coriander stems
50 g Hierba Luisa (lemon verbena) stems
60 g Mucilage honey
50 g Honey
12 g Guar gum
20 g Salt
40 g Lemon juice

Oven bake the pumpkin with the coriander and lemon verbena stems until cooked through and creamy. Process the pumpkin flesh with the honeys, guar gum, salt and lemon juice. Let it cool and reserve.

Pickled Pumpkin Fibres (yield: 3 kg)
3.4 kg Cabello de ángel green squash
1 kg Water
3 g Coriander seeds
3 g Black peppercorns
3 g Cumin seeds
100 g Honey
2 g Cloves
1 kg White vinegar
1 kg Rice vinegar

1 Through a small hole, fill the pumpkin with the coriander and cumin seeds, black peppercorns and cloves. Bake at 160°C for 90 minutes. When cool enough to handle, cut open the pumpkin and remove the fibres. **2** Heat the water, white vinegar, rice vinegar and honey in a saucepan to make a pickling liquid. Let cool and reserve. **3** Immerse the pumpkin fibres in the cooled liquid and allow to pickle for 24 hours before using.

5 Choclos

1 servi

MOMENT FIVE

INGREDIENTS
1 Quinua tamal
5 g Escabeche sauce
40 g Choclo foam
5 g Baby choclo, sliced into rounds
1 g Dried choclo husk ash
5 g Fried choclo silk
10 g Choclo corn nuts

PREPARATION
1 Set the tamal on a serving stone and fashion a small hole in the tamal. **2** Fill the hole with the escabeche sauce. **3** Arrange the baby choclo rounds and the corn nuts atop the sauce. **4** Cover the tamal and toppings with choclo foam. 5 Dust the dish with the husk ash and garnish with fried choclo silk.

————

Quinua Tamil (yield: 100 tamales)
2 kg Red onion, chopped
5 g Garlic confit, minced
8 g Vegetable shortening
3 kg Choclo kernels, puréed
3 kg Quinua, cooked
2 g Black pepper
4 g Sugar
6 g Salt
5 g Dried choclo husk ash
3 g Oregano
340 g Chicken escabeche sauce
350 g Vegetable oil
Fresh corn husks, as needed

1 Heat the vegetable shortening and vegetable oil in a large pot and make a sofrito by sautéing the onion and confit garlic. **2** When the onions have softened, mix in the puréed choclo and stir constantly until cooked. **3** Mix in the quinua, add the ash for colour, and season with the pepper,sugar, salt and oregano. **4** Weigh the tamales to 32 grams each. **5** Fill the tamales with cooked quinua and escabeche sauce. **6** Wrap the tamales in fresh corn husks and cook in plenty of boiling water for 40 minutes.

Choclo Foam (yield:1.8 kg)
1 kg Fresh choclo kernels, cooked
200 g Sofrito (see previous recipe)
160 g Butter
1 kg Cream
40 g Sugar
10 g Salt
500 g Reserved choclo water

1 Add all the ingredients to a pot except the choclo butter and salt and cook for 20 minutes without bringing to a boil. **2** Liquify the cooked ingredients with the choclo water and season with salt.

Chicken Escabeche Sauce (yield: 3.2 kg)
3 kn Chicken stock
1.6 kg White onion, mirepoix cut
300 g Ají amarillo (yellow chilli pepper), julienned
70 g Confit garlic
1 kg Ají amarillo paste
150 g Panca chilli paste
100 g Vinegre
50 g Sugar
10 g Bay leaves
150 g Vegetable oil
Xanthan gum, as needed
6 g Salt

1 Sauté the onion and julienned ají amarillo in oil over medium-high heat. **2** Add the paste and brown. **3** Add the chicken stock and remaining ingredients. **4** Use an immersion blender to liquify, allow to thicken a bit, and strain. **5** Adjust the seasoning.

6 Peces amazónicos

1 serv.

MOMENT SIX

INGREDIENTS
1 Plantain taco
1 Fritter
10 g Paiche ham
1 Varnished Carachama (armoured catfish)

PREPARATION
Assemble each step on its presentation ware.

———

Fritter Batter (yield: 1 kg)
350 g Eggs
500 g Flour
24 g Sugar
350 g Water
24 g Honey
5 g Panca chilli ash

1 Steadily mix the egg and water in a bowl, then add the flour in two parts, followed by the panca ash. Finish by adding the sugar and honey. **2** Mix until the batter is uniform, then transfer it to a whipping syphon with 2 gas cartridges. Allow the batter to rest for 8 hours before using.

Barbecue Sauce Base (yield: 1.2 kg)
610 g Chancaca syrup
1 kg Ketchup
760 g Vinegar
50 g Sillao (soy) sauce
12 g Garlic powder
1 g Ground cumin
1 g Cayenne pepper
180 g Confit garlic
2 g Tabasco sauce
1 g Ground black pepper
16 g Salt
100 g Water

1 Add all the ingredients to a saucepan and cook over medium heat for 1 hour. **2** Strain and set aside.

Tucupi Barbecue Sauce (yield: 1.8 kg)
1.2 kg Barbecue sauce base
600 g Tucupi sauce (from cassava)
2 g Culantro (not coriander)

Use a mortar to crush the culantro into a paste, then mix it in a bowl with the other ingredients. Strain.

Plantain Paper (yield: 8.21 kg)
7.58 kg Ripe plantains
5 kg Water

1 Let the plantains ripen until the peels are dark brown. **2** Peel and cu the plantain, add them to a pot with the water, cook for about 30 minute until the plantain is cooked through completely. **3** Transfer the plantai to a Thermomix and process for abo 4 minutes at maximum temperatur until smooth. **4** Spread the hot plan tain on a Silpat and dehydrate for 8 hours at 60°C. **5** Cut the resulting paper with a 7cm-diameter pastry cu ter and set aside until ready to fry. **6** Fry at 160°C until golden brown, move while still pliable and set them on taco shell moulds until crispy.

Gamitana (tambaqui) (yield: 5 servings)
180 g Gamitana
15 g Tucupí barbecue sauce
30 g Gamitana skin
5 g Butter
5 g Salt
10 g Honey
5 g Purple aster petals
5 Wood skewers

1 Cut the gamitana loin into 4 cm long x 1.5 cm wide x 1.5 cm high pieces. **2** Clean the gamitana skin and, ing a weight to keep the skin flat, grill it with salt and butter until golden an crispy. **3** Sear the gamitana loin on both sides, basting it with tucupi barbecue sauce. Remove from the grill a place the skin on top, lay the purple as ter decorated skewers across the loin

Paiche Taco (yield: 1 serving)
2 Plantain taco shells
5 g Chalaca salsa
1 g Culantro (not coriander)
1 g Salt
1 g Lemon juice
1 g Charapita chilli
5 g Tucupi barbecue sauce
5 g Minced cured pork
5 g Paiche loin
3 g White aster petals
5 g Plantain purée

1 Mix together the chalaca, chopped culantro, salt, lemon juice, charapita chilli, tucupi barbecue sauce, minced cured pork, sautéed and minced paiche loin, and set aside. **2** Place the plantain tacos on their base, add a thin line of plantain purée across the bottom of the taco, followed by the mixed filling and finished with a carefully arranged covering of aster petals. Set aside.

Fritter Filling (yield: 300 g)
80 g Cured pork, minced and fried
5 g Culantro
2 g Salt
200 g Amazonion dressing
2 g Pickled charapita chilli

Thoroughly mix the ingredients together and set aside to fill the fritter.

Amazonian Dressing (yield: 1.29 kg)
2 kg White onion, feather-cut
2 g Charapita chilli
50 g Miskina herb
150 g Culantro
3 L Cured cecina stock (dried pork smoked with Amazon herbs)
100 g Vegetable oil
150 g Confit garlic

1 Sauté the onions with the confit garlic. **2** Add the miskina until the onion is golden brown. **3** Slowly begin adding in the broth and letting it reduce. **4** Add the culantro and charapita while adding the broth. When the liquid has evaporated, remove the culantro and charapita and process the mix until it's a uniformly smooth sauce.

7 Alpaca

MOMENT SEVEN

1 servi

INGREDIENTS
16 g Tuber purée
16 g Alpaca meat
4 g Olluco crisps
1 g Chilli powder
18 g Tapioca pearls
70 g Cuchuro (nostoc)
30 g Andean herb sauce
1 g Coriander flowers
1 Potato presentation
20 g Uchucuta (yellow chilli sauce)

PRESENTATION
1 Plate the tuber purée; we use a potato presentation. **2** Followed by the alpaca glazed in demi-glace with olluco crisps on top. **3** Dust with chilli powder and add tapioca pearls. **4** Finish by adding cushuro and garnish with coriander flowers. **5** Fill the top of the potato presentation with the uchucuta sauce and garnish with fresh oxalis.

———

Liquified Andean Herbs (yield: 500 g)
500 g Chincho
500 g Muña
500 g Paico
500 g Huacatay
400 g Filtered Water

1 Remove the leaves from their stems and wash the herbs. **2** Blanch the herbs and shock in an icebath. **3** Blend all the ingredients with the water, pass through a fine strainer and set aside.

Alpaca Stock (yield: 10 L not)
5 kg Alpaca strip loin meat
750 g White onions
600 g Carrots
400 g Celery
250 g Leeks
10 kg Water
3 kg Peruvian white potato (or use Atlantic)

1 Put all the ingredients in a pot except the white potato. Simmer for about 8 hours until the meat is tender and the liquid reduced by half. Set aside. **2** Strain all the broth and reserve the alpaca meat. **3** Add the 3 kilos of mirepoix-cut potato into the 5 litres of stock, let it cook for about 40 minutes, then pass it through a fine strainer.

Demi-glace (yield: 4 kg)
11 kg Beef bones
15 kg Pork trotters
750 g Onions
600 g Carrots
800 g Celery
250 g Leeks
50 L Water
50 g Honey
100 g Butter
800 g Coriander stems

1 Mirepoix-cut all the vegetables, transfer to an oven pan and roast at 220°C to brown. **2** Brown all the bones and pig's trotters at the same temperature. **3** Once browned, transfer the vegetables and bones to a professional kitchen-sized stock pot alon with 50 litres of water and cook for 12 hours. Strain through a fine sieve the skim off the fat. **4** Transfer to a pot, reduce to 4 litres, then strain and reserve.

Andean Herb Sauce (yield 1.2 kg)
1 L Alpaca shoulder rib stock
250 g Liquified Andean herbs
10 g Chuño (black freeze-dried potato
15 g salt

Transfer the ingredients to a saucepa and stir in the grated chuño until the texture is consistent. Adjust the seasoning and set aside.

Tuber Purée (yield: 1.5 kg)
1 kg Olluco purée
200 g Cassava, cooked
300 g Yellow potato, cooked

1 Put all the ingredients in a saucepan and mix over medium heat until uniformly combined. **2** Process in a blender then pass it through a strainer and reserve.

Olluco Crisps (140 g)
1 kg Ollucos
5 g Salt

1 Use a mandoline to slice the ollucos. **2** Blanch the ollucos in salted water, then dry thoroughly. **3** Fry the slices in oil in a pot or large saucepan. Sprinkle on the salt when they're removed.

Olluco Purée (yield: 3 kg)
2.5 kg Ollucos
500 g Aderezo base (like a sofrito, it's garlic, red onion
and yellow chilli sautéed in oil or lard)
120 g Butter
400 g Yellow chilli paste
400 g Huamantanga potatoes
180 g Chicken stock
10 g Confit garlic

1 Add the aderezo base and chilli paste to a large pot and cook golden brown. **2** Once golden, add the mirepoix-cut ollucos, stir constantly and add the chicken stock, then add the mirepoix-cut potatoes and continue stirring until everything is cooked through. **3** Adjust the seasoning, process in a food processor, then strain and set aside.

Chilli Powder (yield: 350 g)
2.5 kg Ollucos
350 g Yellow chilli paste
350 g Panca chilli paste
100 g Vinegar
10 g Salt

1 Slice and blanch the ollucos, then allow them to drain. **2** Cook the pastes, vinegar and salt in a saucepan for about 15 minutes until they're well mixed and browned, then add the blanched olluco. **3** Continue cooking until all the ingredients are integrated, then spread the mixture on a silicone mat and bake at 55°C for 12 hours. **4** Process the mixture in a blender, then pass through a fine sieve.

Uchucuta Sauce (yield: 1.3 kg)
1 kg Locoto chillies
400 g Onion
200 g Confit garlic
300 g Fresh cheese, crumbled
10 g Huacatay
150 g Cancha Chullpi (corn nuts)

1 Remove the ribs and seeds from the locoto chillies, then wash them 3 times. Blanch the chillies to minimise their heat, peel them and set aside. **2** Mirepoix-cut the onion and sauté in a saucepan until translucent, then add the locoto and continue cooking until cooked through. Set aside to cool. **3** Once cooled, mix in the garlic, huacatay and cancha chullpi, adjust the seasoning and add the crumbled cheese. Refrigerate.

8 Amazónico

MOMENT EIGHT

1 servin

INGREDIENTS

5 g Limón rugoso (rough lemon) purée
10 g Candied macambo seeds
15 g Amazónica cream
5 g Mango, brunoise-cut
20 g Arazú cloud
10 g Copoazú jellies
5 g Honeycomb
10 g Copoazú sorbet
5 Yellow daisy petals

PREPARATION

Place the rough lemon puree at the base of the plate, then the candied macambo seeds followed by fresh brunoise-cut mango, cover everything with the Amazónica cream and add the arazá cloud. Garnish with the jellies, honeycomb, the daisy petals and finish with the sorbet.

————

Limón Rugoso (rough lemon) Purée (yield: 3.5 kg)

3 kg Rough lemon skin (no pith)
1 kg Sugar
1 kg Rough lemon juice
500 g Butter, chilled

Remove the lemon peel (skin only, no pith) and blanch 3 times. First boil: Place the skin in boiling, wait about 5 minutes until the water turns dark green, strain and discard the water. Second boil: Boil the skin again for 5 minutes in fresh water. Strain and discard the water. Third boil: This time boil the skin for 25 minutes, then strain and discard the water. Weigh out 1 kilogram of the cooked skin and transfer to a Thermomix with the sugar and juice and process at 50°C. Once processed, mix in the chilled butter.

Candied Macambo Seeds (yield: 400 g)

300 g Macambo (related to cacao) seeds
150 g Sugar
Water, as needed
20 g Butter

1 Clean the macambo seeds, weigh them out and toast them. **2** Heat the sugar to a saucepan with enough water to dissolve the sugar. Bring it to the point of turning to syrup, when the sugar has dissolved, and mix in the macambo seeds. **3** Continue stirring until caramelised and the seeds are completely covered. **4** Remove from the heat, add a cube of butter, and spread the seeds out on a silicone mat to cool.

Amazonica Cream (yield: 500g)

286 g Cream
180 g Cream cheese
110 g Melipona bee honey
75 g Cacao mucilage honey
1.5 Isinglass sheets

1 Beat the cream until it's the consistency of yoghurt. Refrigerate. **2** Combine the cheese and honeys in a stand mixer. **3** Hydrate the isinglass. **4** Continue mixing until it's smooth and uniform, then slowly add in isinglass and mix it in thoroughly. **5** Remove from the mixer and fold in the cream.

Arazá Cloud (yield: 500 g)

300 g Arazá pulp
200 g Sugar
44 g Albumin powder
3 g Citric acid
120 g Dextrose

With the exception of the dextrose, combine all the ingredients and beat until foamy, then add the dextrose an continue beating until it looks like a meringue.

Copoazú Jellies (yield: 600 g)

500 g Copoazú pulp
150 g Sugar
45 g Isinglass
124 g water

1 Combine the copoazú, sugar and water in a mixer. While mixing, slowly add and mix in the isinglass, and continue mixing until the mixture is uniform. **2** Spread the mixture onto non-stick sheet-lined trays. **3** Divide into 1 cm x 1 cm pieces.

Honeycomb (yield: 400 g)

270 g Sugar
315 g Glucose
120 g Melipona bee honey
24 g Baking soda

1 Except for the baking soda, add the ingredients to a saucepan and continue stirring until the contents reach 120°C. **2** When the contents reach 157°C, mix in the baking soda and stir vigorously until it rises. Remove from the heat. **3** Spread the mix onto a silicone mat and allow to cool.

Copoazú Sorbet (yield: 2 kg)

800 g Filtered water
400 g Sugar
118 g Dextrose
9.5 g Sorbet stabiliser
1 kg Copoazú pulp

1 Begin heating the water, sugar and dextrose in a pot. Once the contents reach 45°C, mix in the stabiliser and bring the heat up to 85°C. **2** Transfer to a container, let cool then mix in the copoazú pulp.

9 Tumbo

MOMENT NINE

1 servir

INGREDIENTS
1 Tumbo presentation
20 g Tumbo sorbet
4 g Pampanis (tagetes) streusel
10 g Yoghurt foam
7 Passion fruit seeds
2 Caigua confit
20 g Tumbo gel

PREPARATION
Arrange the tumbo presentation and follow with tumbo sorbet, pampanis streusel and caigua confit. Cover the base with yoghurt foam then cover with tumbo gel, working from the periphery to the centre, and decorate with 7 passion fruit seeds in a zigzag pattern.

————

Tumbo sorbet
830 g Filtered water
340 g Sugar
4 g Sorbet/ice cream stabiliser
160 g Passion fruit
540 g Tumbo juice

1 Weigh out the filtered water, sugar and dextrose and combine in a pot. This is the sorbet base. Weigh out the stabiliser separately along with a few grams of sugar. **2** Transfer the passion fruit and tumbo pulps together in a bowl and set aside. **3** Heat the sorbet base to 45°C, immediately mix in the sorbet stabiliser, then bring the temperature to 85°C while gently and constantly stirring with a whisk. Remove from the heat and continue mixing to dissolve any remaining lumps. Strain into a bowl and set aside until it cools. **4** When the sorbet base has cooled, pour it over the passion fruit and tumbo pulps, mix thoroughly and seal in a vacuum pack without air. **5** Refrigerate for one night then transfer to the freezer. **6** Use 500 g vacuum pack bags. **7** For use, process in an ice cream turbine twice.

Pampanis Streusel (yield: 250 g)
80 g Butter, unsalted
80 g Sugar
12 g Ground pampanis
80 g Pastry flour

1 Dry the pampanis at 60°C then process and pass through a sieve. Set aside. **2** Weigh out the butter, sugar and cream and beat in a stand mixer. Once integrated, mix in the dry ingredients. **3** Spread the mixture on a silicone mat and bake at 180°C for about 14 minutes. Move the dough every 4 minutes from the sides inwards until it's baked through and picked up the correct colour. **4** Once cooled, transfer to a container and set aside.

Caigua Confit (yield: 160 g)
4 g Caigua fruit
600 g Water
190 g Sugar
20g Lime zest (4 limes)

1 Brunoise-cut the caigua. **2** Combine the water and sugar in a saucepan to make a syrup. When the sugar has completely dissolved, transfer it to a bowl and allow it to cool **3** Blanch the caigua until it's al dente, about 2 to 3 minutes, cut the cooking in an inverted bain-marie (ice water bath) then drain. **4** Transfer the cooked caigua to the cooled syrup and mix in the lime zest.

Yoghurt Foam (yield: 625 g)
400 g Plain yoghurt
30 g Icing sugar
200 g Cream

1 Weigh out the yoghurt, icing sugar and cream, mix thoroughly. **2** Transfer the mixture to a vacuum bag and freeze. **3** Defrost before using and transfer to a whipping syphon with 2 charges.

Tumbo Gel (yield: 280 g)
250 g Tumbo juice
30 g Sugar
3 g Guar gum

1 Use a mixer to combine the tumbo juice and sugar in a bowl. **2** In order to avoid lumps, add the guar gum without pausing and continue mixing until homogenised. **3** Reserve.

10 Tunta

MOMENT TEN

1 servi

INGREDIENTS
1 Osmotic yacón
1 g Purple aster petals (montecasino)
2 g Lime zest

PREPARATION
1 Square and thinly slice the yacón. **2** Garnish with lime zest, 8 drops of lime pulp and 6 Montecasino petals.

————

Osmotic Yacón
3 kg Water
2.5 kg Honey
90 g Ascorbic acid
14 kg Yacón tubers
Additional water for soaking

1 Peel the yacón and soak them in water and the ascorbic acid to prevent oxidation. **2** Combine the honey and measured water and bring the mixture to 30° to dilute the honey. **3** Fill vacuum bags with 4 to 5 tubers, depending on their size, and add the diluted honey. **4** Vacuum seal with zero air and cook in a steam oven at 90°C for 45 to 50 minutes, again, depending on the sizes of the yacóns.

————

Tunta (White sun-dried potato) 1 Serving 1 Mochi tunta

1 Arrange the tunta on the service ware. **2** Arrange the garnished yacón on the serving stone.

————

Chincho Ice Cream (yield: 1 kg)
650 g Milk
100 g Evaporated milk
100 g Cream
100 g Sugar
30 g Powdered milk
4 g Ice cream stabiliser
30 g Dextrose
60 g Chincho (an Andean aromatic grass)

1 Remove the chincho leaves from the tough stems, then wash and dry them before weighing. **2** Weigh out the milk, evaporated milk, cream, sugar and dextrose and transfer them to a pot. **3** Weigh out the ice cream stabiliser, add a pinch of sugar and set aside. **4** Heat the mixture to 45°C, add the ice cream stabiliser, and gently but continuously whisk until it reaches 85°C. **5** Remove from the heat, allow the mixture to cool for 7-10 minutes, then mix in the chincho leaves and let them steep for 15 minutes. **6** After 15 minutes, strain gently and let the infused cream cool. **7** Divide the cream into 500-gram portions and refrigerate for a night so that it develops body. Process in an ice cream turbine.

Mochi Dough (yield: 20 pieces)
240 g Tunta flour
150 g Sugar
354 g Water
Rice flour, as needed

1 Weigh out all the ingredients except the rice flour and mix them in a microwave-safe container, cover and cook in the microwave for 2.50 minutes, uncover and stir the ingredients thoroughly. **2** Repeat the cooking twice at 1 minute 30 seconds, stirring thoroughly after each time. **3** Use a sifter or sieve to spread the rice flour over a work surface, place the dough on top and use a rolling pin to roll out the dough, being careful that it doesn't stick to the surface nor is it allowed to cool. Roll out to 5-mm thickness, use a pastry cutter to cut circles, then roll out the circles a little more with the a of a little more rice flour. To reserve, place each dough circle on a non-stic food separator sheet, cover with another sheet, and repeat.

Tunta Mochi (yield: 1 serving)
23 g Chincho ice cream
1 Mochi disc
1 g Black ash

1 Make balls of chincho ice cream and place them on a tray lined with cling film and freeze at -18°C. **2** Line the bottom of a freezer-safe container with a non-stick sheet(s). Then lin a try with small non-stick sheets and place the mochi discs on top. Place a ball of ice cream on each disc and seal the dough around it, removing any excess dough as you're handling it. **3** Quickly move the balls to the freezer container with the ball closur facing down.

11 Mucílago

1 servir

MOMENT ELEVEN

INGREDIENTS
30 g Cacao tea
9 g Pacay, fresh and seeded
4 g mucilage sorbet
1 sprig Canada goldenrod flower

PREPARATION
1 Add the cacao tea to one half of the pacay shell, then cover it with cocoa husk foam. **2** Arrange a Canada goldenrod flower for decoration, and follow with the pacay filled with the sorbet.

————

Cacao Tea (yield: 1.9 kg)
5 Cacao pods, whole
280 g Sugar
180 g Mucilage honey
3 L Water

1 Wash the cocoa pod and cut open. **2** Place in a pot and add water and cool on a medium heat until boiling, then lower the flame. **3** Let it reduce until the infusion has a gummy consistency, then strain, add sugar and mucilage honey to flavour.

Mucilage Sorbet (yield: 2.8 kg)
80 g Water
280 g Mucilage
200 g Sugar
300 g Dextrose
16 g Sorbet stabiliser
1.94 kg Mucilage
40 g Lemon juice
40 g Mucilage honey

1 Weigh out the first five ingredients (water, mucilage, sugar, dextrose and stabiliser) and, except for the stabiliser, combine in a pot. Keep the stabiliser aside. **2** Weigh out the last three ingredients (mucilage, lemon juice and mucilage honey) and combine them in a mixing bowl. **3** Bring the sorbet base (the first four ingredients) to 45°C on a direct heat, add the sorbet stabiliser, beat gently and thoroughly until it reaches 85°C, then remove from heat, strain into a mixing bowl and set aside. **4** Once the base is cold, mix in the mucilage, lemon juice and honey to the base, set aside. **5** Once cooled, seal the bowl and let it sit overnight in the fridge. **6** Freeze the mixture and use an ice cream turbine (mixer) before serving.

Cacao Foam (yield: 2 kg)
2 kg Filtered water
100 g Sugar
70 g Cacao husk
46 g Lecithin

1 In a pot, bring the water to 85°C, add the husk and the sugar, remove from the heat and let it rest for 25 minutes. **2** Strain the liquid and mix in the lecithin.

SECTION_7_THE

AR

Pisco, Peru's elixir

Raúl Otero

Pisco isn't just an alcoholic beverage: for us, it signifies terroir and people, many of whom are from Santa Cruz, the village located just 300 metres from the vineyard and distillery. That is what gives us a unique identity.

While my brother Jaime wants to conquer the world through gastronomy, I want to conquer the world with our family project, Bodega San Nicolás Pisco 1615.

In the mid-16th century, much of Latin America was under Spanish rule and Peru was the colonialists' designated headquarters. The Spaniards brought many of their traditions halfway across the world, including mistela or wine for Mass. In order for them to comply with their essential religious ceremonies, their Jesuit priests needed to start cultivating grapes. An industry was born.

Listán Prieto, also known as Negra Criolla, was one of the first varieties to reach the Americas, and today it's one of the eight-strong cast permitted to produce pisco in Peru. Vineyard cultivation was initiated across many viceroyalties, including the Lanchas Valley – home to the Santa Cruz de Lancha monastery ruins – and that is precisely where Bodega San Nicolás Pisco 1615's vineyards are located.

But, Peruvian wine quality was surprisingly high, so much so that it was seen as a competitive threat to Spain's own production. King Felipe III started to discourage production but distilling became a viable solution.

In his heralded chronicles to the Spanish king, the writer Felipe Guamán Poma de Ayala recounted developments and news in the colonies. In 1615, he published 'Nueva crónica y buen gobierno' (New Chronicle and Good Governing), and talked up key valleys: one of those was our very own Lanchas Valley.

At Bodega San Nicolás Pisco 1615, we want to return to tradition while creating an identity – and share pisco with the world.

Pisco has long been relevant during the centuries both before and after Peru's independence in 1821. By that notable date, an array of private entities were distilling and exporting their own products, which led to a golden age of pisco exports to the USA in the 19th century.

Our country has been constructed by people of many origins, a fusion of mestizo and Spanish (as well as other European) cultures that have blended with Indigenous cultures. For me, pisco represents identity diversity that we Peruvians are still learning to understand.

When our family bought the bodega in 2011 – as Jaime recounts earlier in the chapter – we first studied the complex sandy and saline terroir that millions of years earlier was the ocean bed. Then we selected the four grapes that would grow best here, just 10 kilometres from the ocean, that we also consider to represent the future of pisco:

While Quebranta is the most widely cultivated variety in Peru, it's very adaptable and the best suited to our soil. The least aromatic, it works well in cocktails, plus it has a great body. Torrontel, meanwhile, is highly aromatic and also boasts herbaceous organoleptic notes. Italia is the most aromatic of pisco's eight permitted varieties with citrus notes adding complexity to its profile.

The fourth grape, Albilla, is a halfway point between the last two, and the aromatic profiles of these former three are versatile when it comes to making cocktails, such as our revered Pisco Sour (a 4-1-1- concoction shaken with egg white and lemon juice then strained, with a few Angostura drops as a garnish, that was first created in Lima in 1916, and the Pisco Punch that was invented in San Francisco at the end of the 19th century.

Our grapes bear high salinity and high minerality, which end up creating a pisco with marked characteristics.

Pisco isn't just an alcoholic beverage: for us, it signifies terroir and people, many of whom are from Santa Cruz, the village located just 300 metres from the winery. That is what gives us a unique identity and our mission as a bodega is to create pisco's second wave – and that starts with inspiring guests at Mayta.

Cocktail Recipes

As the bar is such a vital part of the experience at Mayta, I wanted to share nine cocktail recipes – three with pisco, three made with innovative distillates that we create in house, and three alcohol-free ones – for guests. We take the same approach in the bar as we do in the kitchen, championing the use of every last piece of pith and skin or drop of juice, and guests will savour ingredients such as quinua, tumbo and mucilage but in a liquid format. The bartenders draw from more than 200 spirits, including seven of our family pisco, and around 30 Peruvian distillates. Do note that the non-alcoholic cocktails are designed to be paired with the Experiencia Mayta Menu.

While Mayta 1.0 had a strong concept when it came to mixing drinks, I further understood the importance of fantastic cocktails in a restaurant setting once my family started distilling pisco.

Pisco is close to my heart for two reasons. First, it's Peru's national spirit and second, my family has its own distillery and brand, Bodega San Nicolás Pisco 1615, and that makes this distilled wine an even more special beverage. This is why the bar has always taken a central role in Mayta.

It's the first thing you see when you enter the restaurant, framed by jars of macerating fruits, housing our in-house still and a well-polished espresso machine.

Drinks begin as well as close a dining experience because you start with a beverage, probably an appetite-stimulating apéritif – such as Pacha, which uses Pisco 1615 Quebranta redistilled with horsetail, muña and hierba luisa and finish with one, most likely a coffee or perhaps an herbal infusion such as muña, which is excellent for the digestive system. I've always appreciated how vital it is to have a strong drinks programme and the importance of allowing guests additional moments to relax from day-to-day distractions with a cocktail or alcohol-free drink. It indicates the start of the EXPERIENCIA MAYTA MENU.

Personally I'm a chilcano fan, a tall drink of pisco mixed with ginger ale, and I love its versatility because it's easy to boost it with floral, citrus or fruit notes.

At the original Mayta, we developed a solid pisco list that included more than 100 chilcano macerations that guests loved, but we raised the game when Mayta 2.0 opened in 2018. After acquiring a copper alembic with a 10-litre capacity, we not only macerated pisco with roots, flowers, leaves, herbs and fruits but we also redistilled it to push the creative boundaries further. The next project was to begin distilling our own alcohol.

As for coffee, we only prepare beans sourced from different regions in Peru then roasted by the Lima specialist Milimétrica.

While guests can enjoy a cocktail at the bar and engage in conversation with head bartender Jhonatan Alvarez Aliaga, we also have a delightful drinks trolley that comes to them at the dining table. It's a way of creating closer contact with our 200-strong global spirits selection, which includes Peruvian interpretations of rum, bourbon, agave, gin and vermouth as well as seven styles of our family pisco.

Aqará, for example, is Peru's answer to tequila, an award-winning Andean agave spirit produced in the Cordilleras Negra y Blanca in the Callejón de Huaylas, at 3,900 metres above sea level. Then, as we Peruvians love ají, we also stock Sinsonte, an apéritif made with seven chilli peppers from Arequipa, as well as Black Whiskey whose mash is made from purple Andean corn.

There's the award-winning Abelino sweet vermouth made with 28 herbs, while the high-elevation Intira gin is distilled with fruits originating from the Cusco region where it's produced. The drinks trolley also pays tribute to ancestral spirits such as Matacuy, a fermented cane juice distillate made in Ollantaytambo in Cusco that is boosted by 25 regional botanicals. Picha, meanwhile, is a coca leaf spirit.

Whatever the drink we prepare for you at the bar or from the trolley, Peruvian identity and spirit – in all the senses – is at its heart.

lbedo De Tumbo
Banana Passionfruit Pith)

Serves 350 ml

GREDIENTS
g Dehydrated tumbo albedo (pith)
g Dehydrated tumbo peel
) ml Tumbo juice
bsp. Yoghurt whey foam

METHOD
Take the tumbo peels and separate the albedo (pith) from the outer skin, then dehydrate them separately. Then soak them in water so as to draw out the tumbo's natural pectin. We add natural yoghurt and tumbo juice to a blender, process for 5 minutes, then strain it. We make a foam with the natural yoghurt's whey.
Serve in a Champagne flute.

Agua De Mar (Sea Water)

Serves 400 ml

INGREDIENTS

- 0 g Sea lettuce
- 0 ml Hot water
- g Golden pineapple
- g Maras salt

METHOD

First, place the sea lettuce in hot water and, once it has cooled, strain it. Peel the golden pineapple, slice it up then place in a food processor with the sea lettuce. Strain this mixture and add a little salt until it reaches the point of umami.

We serve Agua de Mar in our bespoke Coral Martini glass and pair it with the Paracas course.

?apa Seca
(Dried Potato)

Serves 1 L

NGREDIENTS

00 g Sea lettuce
00 ml Hot water
0 g Golden pineapple
g Maras salt

METHOD

First, place the sea lettuce in hot water and, once it has cooled, strain it. Peel the golden pineapple, slice it up then place in a food processor with the sea lettuce. Strain this mixture and add a little salt until it reaches the point of umami.

We serve Agua de Mar in our bespoke Coral Martini glass and pair it with the Paracas course.

Marujito

Yield 120 ml

OR THE PISCO SOUR CREAM
eld 1 L

GREDIENTS
) ml Pisco 1615 Quebranta
30 ml Simple syrup
3 g Albumin powder
.0 ml Lemon juice
g Xanthan gum
0 ml Egg whites

ETHOD
ace all the ingredients in a blender r 15 seconds at a medium speed then rain. Place in a whipping syphon, ake and chill for 20 minutes.

FOR THE MARUJITO

INGREDIENTS
60 ml Pisco 1615 Quebranta
60 ml Passionfruit juice
120 ml Ginger ale
15 ml Simple syrup
8 Muña leaves
Pisco Sour Cream to finish
Rose petal dust

METHOD
In a highball glass, add the muña leaves, four ice cubes, then add the pisco, passionfruit juice, simple syrup and ginger ale, mix to chill the ingredients, then add the Pisco Sour Cream and garnish with a sprinkle of rose petal dust.

The first three cocktails I'm sharing with you are made using our very own Bodega San Nicolás Pisco 1615, which I hope you will enjoy.

Mucílago (Mucilage)

Serves 120 ml

FOR THE COFFEE MUCILAGE
Serves 1 L

INGREDIENTS
1 L Cacao mucilage
00 g Roasted coffee beans

METHOD
Place the mucilage and coffee in a vacuum pack, seal and chill for five days. Remove, then strain and reserve the liquid.

FOR MUCÍLAGO

INGREDIENTS
60 ml Pisco 1615 Mosto Verde
50 ml lemon juice
30 ml simple syrup
60 ml coffee mucilage
30 ml egg white
2 dehydrated rose petals

METHOD
Place all the ingredients in a shaker and dry shake. Then add 5 ice cubes and shake for 10 seconds. Strain twice through a wire strainer then pour into a coupé glass. Decorate with two dehydrated rose petals.

Humo Punch
Smokey Punch)

Serves 150 ml

NGREDIENTS

)5 ml Pisco 1615 Mosto Verde
0 ml Tumbo juice
0 ml Camu camu juice
5 ml Vermouth rosso
ash bitters

METHOD

Place 5 ice cubes in a cocktail shaker then add all the ingredients and shake for 10 seconds. Add 2 ice cubes into the old fashioned glass then pour in the liquid. When we serve Humo Punch to our guests at the table, it is accompanied by dehydrated eucalyptus smoke and a wood bed covered with dry ice that we activate with pineapple perfume and hot water.
Serve in an old fashioned glass.

Cereales
(Cereals)

Serves 90 ml

)R THE KIWICHA ND QUINUA POPCORN

ields 300 ml

NGREDIENTS
50 ml Aperol
0 ml Campari
kg Kiwicha popcorn
50 g Quinua popcorn

IETHOD
lace all the ingredients in a vacuum orage bag and seal for 3 days.

FOR THE KIWICHA AND QUINUA CANDY

Yields 15 units

INGREDIENTS
200 g Sugar
5 g Kiwicha (uncooked)
5 g Quinua (uncooked)

METHOD
In a small saucepan, place the sugar and cook at a low heat until it dissolves, then add the kiwicha and quinua. Pour onto a non-stick silicone mat and leave to cool. Once cooled, slice into small pieces.

FOR CEREALS

INGREDIENTS
15 ml Mayta's roots distillate (yacón, mashwa and maca)
30 ml Kiwicha and quinua infusion
7.5 ml Lemon juice
7.5 ml Degollador (mochero chilli pepper liquor)
Chandon Spritz

METHOD
Add 4 ice cubes to the martini glass then add the roots distillate, kiwicha and quinua infusion then top off with Chandon Spritz. Garnish, with the kiwicha and quinua candy.

The following three cocktails use our own liqueurs that Jhonatan and the bar team create in house, allowing them to employ their skills to create brand-new flavours such as bitters and distillates made from roots.

;ushuro and Strawberry

Serves 90 ml

)R THE STRAWBERRY AND HONEY

NGREDIENTS
)0 ml Amazon melipona honey
)0 ml Strawberries
) ml White wine vinegar

:ETHOD
ıfuse all the ingredients for four ıys, then strain.

)R THE BLACK TEA

erves 500 ml

NGREDIENTS
3 g Black tea leaves from the Cusco region
)0 ml Hot water

IETHOD
ıfuse the tea.

FOR THE STRAWBERRY AND CUSHURO SHRUB

Yields 700 gr

INGREDIENTS
1 kg Strawberries
600 g White sugar
700 ml White wine vinegar
1 kg Cushuro

METHOD
Add the white wine vinegar, sugar and strawberries into a saucepan over low heat. Once the sugar has dissolved, remove from the heat and leave to cool. Once the shrub has cooled, add the cushuro and leave to steep for 3 days in a sealed container.

FOR CUSHURO AND STRAWBERRY

INGREDIENTS
15 ml Mayta's citrus distillate (rough skinned lemon, orange, sanky cactus fruit)
22 ml Strawberry mix
2 Drops orange bitters
15 ml Aqará Rito agave distillate
90 ml Tonic water
60 ml Ginger ale
4 Pickled cushuro spheres

METHOD
Place a stick of ice in an old fashioned glass, add all the ingredients then cool. Garnish with pickled cushuro, served on a wooden spoon.

Ierbal and Cacao

Serves 120 ml

R THE AMARO WITH CACAO NIBS

rves 120 ml

GREDIENTS

30 ml Amaro

0 g Cacao nibs

2 g Orange skin

g Cardamom

3 g Cat's claw leaves

FOR HERBAL AND CACAO

INGREDIENTS

15 ml Mayta's herbal distillate

75 ml Cacao nib amaro

2 Drops cacao bitters

1 Mayta ice cube

METHOD

Add 6 ice cubes to a mixing glass and stir for 10 seconds, remove the excess water with a wire strainer. Add all the liquid ingredients and stir for 10 more seconds, then in an old fashioned glass, place the ice cube stamped with the Mayta logo, then pour the mixed ingredients into the glass. Garnish with the cacao candy.

The spirits of Peru

Besides championing our family piscos and innovating to create our own distillates, we also hold dear Peru's ever-growing family of spirits that seek to share Peruvian identity, whether it's through gin, vodka, vermouth and whiskey. We put around 30 such beverages with a special spotlight on the drinks trolley, so that guests can get closer to these special liquors and bartenders can share more information about their origins. These are some of our favourites.

On the drinks trolley

AQARÁ
Andean distillate made with penca, cabuya and maguey agave in Caraz, 2,256 metres above sea level.

AQHA REAL
The traditional chicha de jora corn beer is upgraded by fortification.

AVELINO
Sweet vermouth made with 28 herbs sourced from different regions of Peru.

CAÑA ALTA
Sugar cane distillate from Destilería Andina in Ollantaytambo.

DEGOLLADOR
Mochero chilli pepper liquor from Trujillo, a city close to the Pacific Ocean in northern Peru.

INTIRA
A gin distilled in the Cusco region made with 24 botanicals.

MATACUY
Ancestral distillate from herbs also made at Destilería Andina in Ollantaytambo, Cusco, 2,792 metres above sea level.

MILLONARIO
An XO rum made in Lambayeque, a northern city close to the Pacific Ocean.

PIKCHA
Coca leaf distillate made in the Cusco region.

SINSONTE
Named after the mockingbird, this chilli pepper apéretif from Arequipa, 2,335 metres above sea level, uses seven Peruvian ajíes.

YUNCAN
Sugar cane distillate made in Huánuco, 1,880 metres above sea level.

MARTIN MILLER'S GIN

SECTION_8_MY_

AYTA_FAMILY

The Mayta family has grown exponentially in 15 years, and today counts almost 80 members, from front of house and administration to line cooks, bartenders and wait staff. Everyone plays their role to keep the restaurant running smoothly and efficiently with purpose and love to ensure our guests fully savour the Mayta dining experience. I'd like to introduce some of my key staff.

Santiago Vidal, *chef*
Santi is my right-hand man in the business world, a very trustworthy person who has worked closely with me in Lima for the past five years and two years ago, started travelling with me. He helps keep me motivated. A confident chef, our line of communication is very direct; we have a very professional partnership.

Felipe Quiroz, *chef de cuisine*
Felipe has worked with us since we opened Mayta 2.0 in December 2018. Starting out as a line cook, he then became the second in command and now, at just just 32, heads the kitchen. A calm person who works well in a team, Felipe has an incredible hand and palate when it comes to seasoning. He also knows how to open channels with love and affection.

The Mayta family

Roberth Alcántara Oyarce, ***head of development***

Roberth started as an intern 5 years ago at Mayta, but his passion for the industry, curiosity about his country, and creativity led him to quickly become a cook. Later, he became a line chef, then Sous Chef, and today, he is the person leading the Development department at Mayta's workshop.

Joan Roig Vilaseca, ***head waiter***

Trained in hospitality at CETT, he has worked in renowned Michelin-starred restaurants such as Vía Veneto, Enoteca, and Can Jubany. His experience led him to London, where he worked with Nacho Manzano at Ibérica and at Arros QD, under Quique Dacosta. His passion for the rise of Latin America's culinary revolution brought him to our country.

The Mayta family, *January 2024*

Roberth Alcantara Oyarce
Angelica Algalobos Aldana
Arjeta Alimi
Jessica Alva Piedra
Jhonatan Alvarez Aliaga
Andre Anticona Vela
Brian Arroyo Acuña
Gheorghe Ballardo Osorio
Barbara Barrios Ramos
Gerald Bouillet Leyton
Fernando Calisaya Córdova
Renzo Callirgos Ibarra
Rodrigo Conde Marcas
Diana Condori Mullisaca
Carol Cordova Natividad
Fernando Coro Pretel
Camila Diaz Alfaro
Nicolas Euribe Gómez
Christofher Flores Sánchez
Sharon Franco Alcarraz
Julio Gamarra Domínguez
Veronica García Sosa
Oscar Gloria Aliaga
Miguel Gonzáles López
Jeremy González Angulo
Lizbany Gormas Amaringo
Daniela Herrera Posada
Rolando Huaman Buitón
Manuel Huanaquiri Azañero
Miguel Hurtado Carrera
Wilson Jara Antaurco
Camila Julca Lalupu
Daniel Ledezma Medina
Leonor Limachi Apaza
Jasmine López Lopez
Jackeline Manallay Azañero
Gabriela Medina Diaz
Ashly Milla López
Jose Alberto Miñano Barauna

Arjeta Alimi, *administrator*

Arjeta is Mayta's administrative leader, the person who puts out fires and counts the pennies, the bridge who connects with the restaurant team every day and links them with human resources. A proactive and tireless worker, she also knows a lot about wine and steps up to work on the floor during service whenever her talents are needed.

Jhonatan Alvarez Aliaga, *head barman*

As our bar manager, Jhonatan is the creative mind behind our cocktails who lovingly curates our pisco collection and undertakes our unique macerations. He works in developing the overall beverages programme. Together, Jhonatan and I put a lot of energy into developing non-alcoholic pairings.

Jose Molina Vicente
Nicol Mondalgo Pomahuacre
Ronald Moscol Orbegoso
Ariel Orellana Mamani
Lorena Palmar Palmar
Bruno Ted Paredes Flores
Oscar Parra AlegriaNerida Pereyra Magallanes De Angeles
Karol Pinedo Lozano
Bryan Prieto Ulloa
Felipe Quiroz Sanchez
Gustavo Luis Sebastián Raáz Perry
Marilyn Ramirez Flores
Jasel Reynaltt Cahuana
Carlos Rojas Amaya
Alvaro Romero Escalante
Vicente Rubiños Balarezo
Walter Salazar Gonzaga
Juan Salinas Diaz
Cesar Salvatierra Mendoza
Grandix Sangama Garcia
Erika Schuler Rosas
Anthony Senador Contreras
Pierre Siguas Ormeño
Elena Silvestre Arteaga
Marschelo Spiridigliozzi Tinedo
Stefano Suarez Reyes
Manuel Talledo Del Castillo
Eylin Tenorio Huaytalla
Luis Torres Norabuena
Michel Torres Romero
Valeria Vásquez Gadea
Martin Vela Pezo
Richard Venegas Alarcon
Santiago Vidal Salcedo

Wilson Jara Antaurco, ***head of production***

The heart of the restaurant, the wonderful Wilson and I have worked together for 20 years, since 2004. A great human being, noble, kind and with spectacular taste, he has worked with me from the very beginning. First he was a cook, then he was head of the kitchen, and now as head of production. Wilson also leads the kitchen: he dishes out all the Mayta DNA and flavours across every line and is a fundamental piece of our puzzle. He truly is a brother to me.

Ronald Carhuas Huamán, head ***sommelier***

Professional sommelier with extensive experience in the gastronomic scene of Lima, working in renowned local restaurants. His passion for wine has led him to explore wine regions in countries such as Germany, France, Spain, the United States, Chile, and Argentina. He is currently a faculty member at Le Cordon Bleu Peru and serves as Head Sommelier at Mayta.

The Pesaque family

Francesca and I are partners in crime.

Parents to three daughters, who have obviously been raised in a busy gastronomy-centred world; Sundays are sacred for our family. We usually go for breakfast to 500 Grados in San Isidro with our eldest Michella who is 14, and twins Isabella and Valentina who are 10, then have lunch either with Francesca's mum or mine.

On Sunday nights, my cooking pasta for the family is sacrament, but I always put together something simple. Pasta is the girls' favourite and I will either prepare a simple tomato sauce or my version of carbonara with egg yolks, butter and a little olive oil. But if there are leftovers from the week's meals such as chicken or vegetables, I might make a chaufa rice dish.

As a couple, Francesca and I have learnt to have a wonderful working relationship that respects and marries both our ambitions. A fashion designer by trade who directs her own brand – she conceived the contemporary uniforms for the front-of-house staff – Fran is competitive and enjoys my success as if it were her own, always spurring me on. Her goals are mine as much as mine are hers.

I will always be grateful to my parents, Patricia and Raúl, for believing in me and supporting me in every possible way, especially emotionally. Raúl isn't just my dad, he's also my business partner. And my seven siblings, too, have always supported me and I thank them for that.

But it's Fran who has helped me to express who I really am.

That's why we are partners in crime.

Acknowledgments

I'd like to thank:

My wife, Francesca, for her support and love, and for making my goals her own. For being my unconditional companion on this journey.

My parents, Patricia and Raúl, for always supporting me, believing in my talent, and for their unconditional support and love throughout this journey.

My daughters, Michella, Isabella, and Valentina, for giving me the strength to keep moving forward, for helping me grow, for being a great reason to push ahead, and for giving me the opportunity to be a father and set an example.

To my siblings, for always being by my side at all times.

And to the Mayta family, to those who have been and are part of it, for their efforts, support, discipline, courage, and unconditional backing on the path to achieving shared goals.

Jaime Pesaque

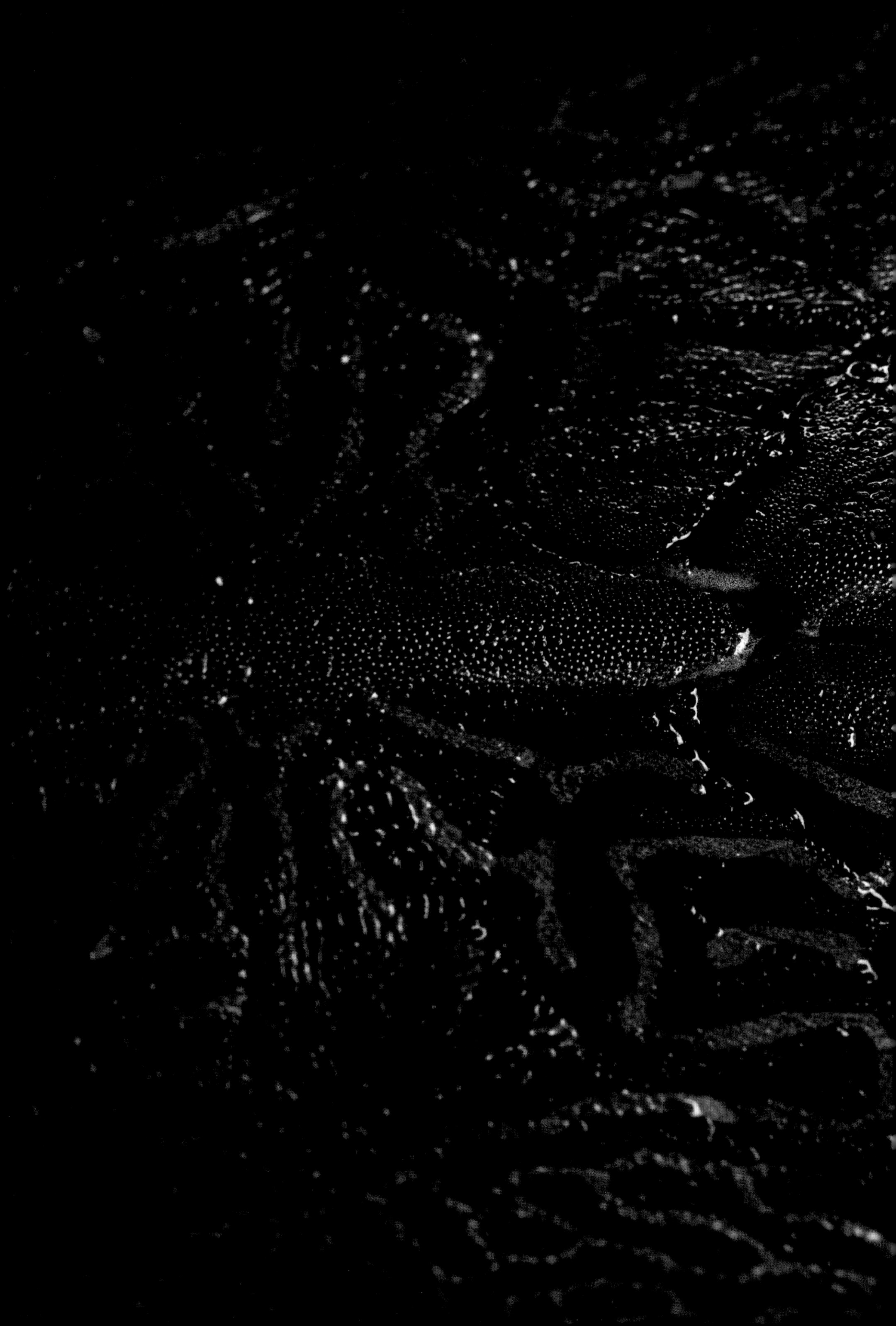

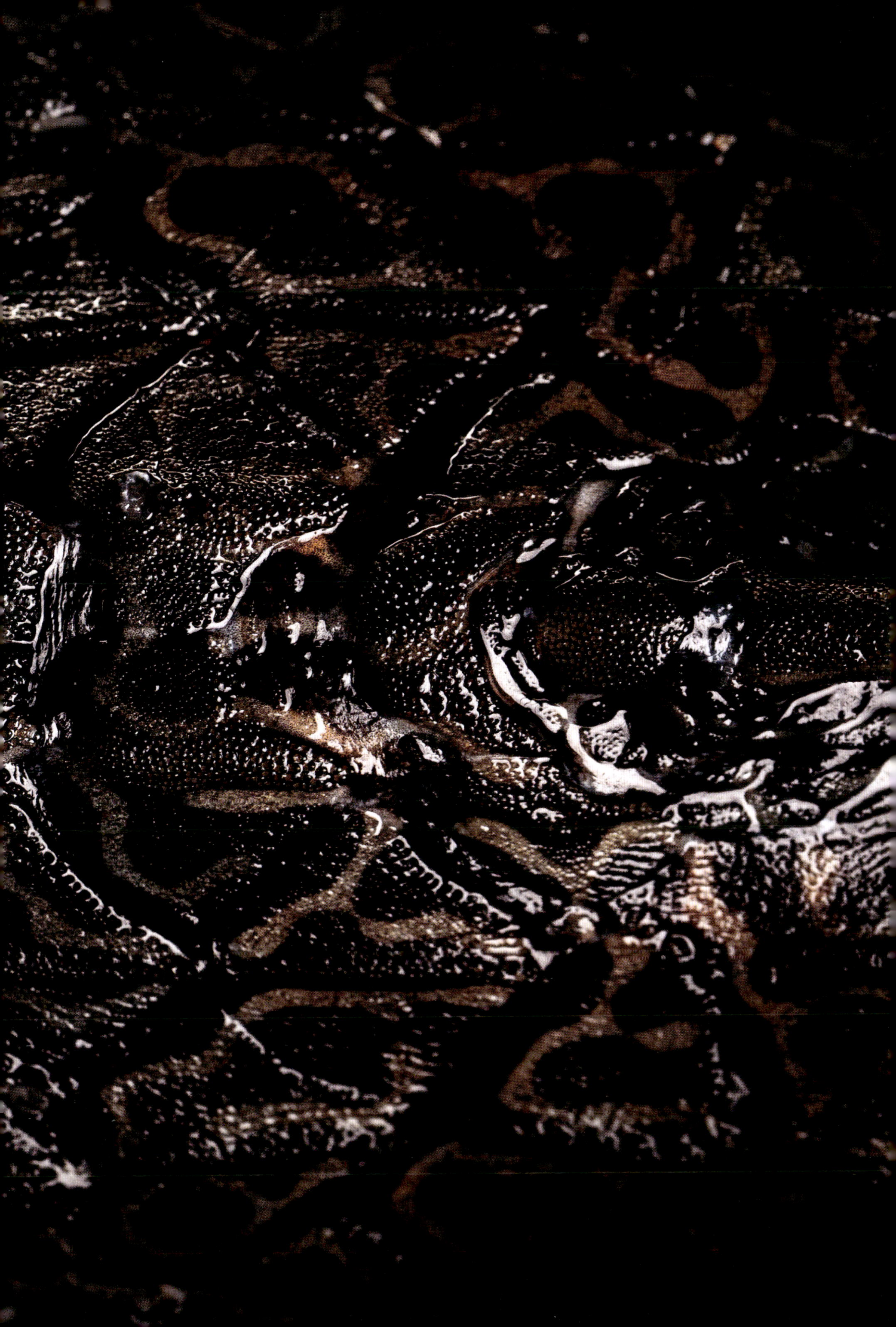

© Mayta
First Edition

Catapulta
Colombia 260 (B1603)
Buenos Aires, Argentina
info@catapulta.nct
www.catapulta.net

General editor **Victoria Blanco**
Art direction and design **Ezequiel Cafaro Studio**
Texts and proofreader **Sorrel Moseley-Williams**

Photographs **Jessica Alva Piedra**
Photography Assistant **Álvaro Loayza Pacheco**
Aerial photography **Alex Avila Gonzales**

Graphic production **Mariana Voglino** y **Verónica Álvarez Pesce**

ISBN 978-987-815-353-7
Printed in China in February, 2025

Pesaque, Jaime
Mayta / Jaime Pesaque
1a ed.
Ciudad Autónoma de Buenos Aires
Catapulta, 2025
248 p. / 27 x 21 cm
1. Libro de entretenimientos
2. Libro de recetas
3. Gastronomía
I. Título
CDD 793.2

ISBN 978-987-815-353-7
9 789878 153537
All rights reserved in accordance with law 11723. Argentine book edition. This book may not be reproduced in its entirety, stored, rented, transmitted or transformed in any form or by any means, without the prior written permission of the publisher. Any violation is punishable by laws 11723 and 25446 of Argentine Copyright Law.